Living in the Afterlife

Experiences from the Soul Place

Michele A. Livingston

ARS METAPHYSICA
an imprint of Sunbury Press, Inc.
Mechanicsburg, PA USA

ARS METAPHYSICA
an imprint of Sunbury Press, Inc.
Mechanicsburg, PA USA

For information about special discounts for bulk purchases, please contact Sunbury Press Orders Dept. at (855) 338-8359 or orders@sunburypress.com.

To request one of our authors for speaking engagements or book signings, please contact Sunbury Press Publicity Dept. at publicity@sunburypress.com.

ISBN: 978-1-62006-041-4 (Trade paperback)

Library of Congress Control Number: 2016941855

FIRST ARS METAPHYSICA EDITION: August 2018

Product of the United States of America
0 1 1 2 3 5 8 13 21 34 55

Set in Bookman Old Style
Designed by Crystal Devine
Cover by Lawrence Knorr
Cover Art by Todd Jumper
Edited by Allyson Gard

Continue the Enlightenment!

In loving memory of my beautiful mother Dorothy,
who from Heaven inspired this book.

I give you my respect and gratitude.

Contents

Other books by Michele A. Livingston

Messages from Beyond:
A Spiritual Guidebook

The True Nature of Love:
Awakening to the Christ Consciousness

Echoes in the Wind:
Messages from the Tribes of the Nation –
Volume 1, The Lakota (Sioux) Nation

Miraculous Encounters:
True stories of Experiences with Angels and
Departed Loved Ones

Visions from Mary

Acknowledgments

I wish to first thank the many souls in Heaven who lovingly and willingly shared their experiences from the afterlife.

Next I acknowledge and thank my true soul-mate and husband, Jon Stroh, for supporting this endeavor every step of the way.

And with gratitude I thank my spiritual friend, Todd Jumper, who created the visionary artwork for the cover of this book.

THE ROSE STILL GROWS BEYOND THE WALL

Near a shady wall a rose once grew,
Budded and blossomed in God's free light,
Watered and fed by morning dew,
Shedding its sweetness day and night.

As it grew and blossomed fair and tall,
Slowly rising to loftier height,
It came to a crevice in the wall,
Through which there shone a beam of light.

Onward it crept with added strength,
With never a thought of fear or pride,
It followed the light through the crevice's length,
And unfolded itself on the other side.

The light, the dew, the broadening view
Were found the same as they were before;
And it lost itself in beauties new,
Breathing its fragrance more and more.

Shall claim of death cause us to grieve,
And make our courage faint or fail?
Nay! Let us faith and hope receive:
The rose still grows beyond the wall.

Scattering fragrance far and wide,
Just as it did in days of yore,
Just as it did on the other side,
Just as it will for evermore.

by A. L. Frink

Introduction

The concept for this book about the "Soul Place" began a few years ago, when I had a surprise visit from my deceased mother, Dorothy. During this communiqué she telepathically stated:

"I feel you should write a book about Heaven—the *soul place* so to speak. I feel it would be needed and well received. Since there are no time parameters here, it can take many years in your earthly time for us to *influence* you with information from our world. Thus the book on 'the place where souls go' (after leaving their physical bodies) is starting to now formulate.

"The word *heaven* conjures angels and clouds—but this is a tangible place, with different levels of energy or frequencies. There are different dimensions with various strata of light. It is quite an ordeal for a soul in a sub-frequency or lower realm position to awaken and graduate to a higher consciousness. This is achieved through the help of heavenly volunteers.

"Heaven is also referred to as the other side, the next world, the spirit realm, the afterlife, the fourth dimension, a higher frequency—just to name a few. It is true that what humans call Heaven is all of the above, yet it is more. It is a place with no space or time. It is a place where a soul's thoughts can manifest into a form of the soul's reality. Because there is no time on this side a soul does not have to wait for anything to occur. Single thoughts can create immediate results of one's desires. Heaven is a place with no limitations. Each positive thought is a creative attempt to be one with the loving force and energy of the Godhead. As each person in the physical world perceives life differently, so do the souls in the fourth dimension. Through their 'thought forms' each soul can create his or her own heaven. Therefore *individual* heavens exist and they are the reality of an individual soul's wishes and desires.

"I will help mentor your book if you like, as I now am starting to help and guide a few writers on the earth plane. You will enjoy writing this book, but you must give yourself copious amounts of time to do so. It will not be a quick fix for people, more of an *awakening* to the reality of another world, which they have forgotten about in their present physical state."

And so began the idea for this book on Heaven. My mother was an English teacher, poet, pianist and had the gift of clairvoyance ("clear seeing" of spirits). Dorothy also received information from precognition dreams, which means *pre-knowing* that an event will happen. She shared with me that my great-grandmother, Jane, was also a visionary in the 1800s, here in Central Pennsylvania. Jane was of the Dunker faith, or "plain people" as they were called. The Dunkers were a very strict religious sect, similar to the Amish, Mennonite and Quaker groups.

I received the gift of vision later in my life at the age of 40, but from the time I was very small I *knew* things were going to happen. Even as a child, people would say that I was an "old soul." When I was only two years old a favorite relative of ours passed away. The memorial service included the viewing of the dead body in an open casket. My mother wasn't convinced that she should expose me to this scenario at such a young age. Yet she agreed to take me, not knowing what my reaction would be. I was later told that everyone was crying, including my mother. When I viewed the lifeless body I said, "Don't worry mama, the *real* person is up there," pointing to the ceiling. This is the story she relayed many times saying I must be an old soul. In addition I told my mother at age three that I was glad I *chose* her to be my mother. I now believe that a soul can actually choose parents in order to learn soul lessons. My half-sister, Doris, was 20 years older than me and very pushy. Once again, at a young age when she was shaking me I stomped my foot and said, "Don't you remember when I was here a long, long time ago?" Well my half-sister ran out of the room screaming, "That kid gives me the creeps!" Later I stunned my fourth grade teacher by recounting details of a story that only she knew.

My initial journey in life started as an artist, when I was creating detailed drawings and paintings around the age of four. Seeing that potential, I was sent to art school and had my first "one-woman show" in sixth grade. I later received a Masters Degree in Education from Penn State University. My art career spanned the next 20 years, including teaching art in public schools, giving private art lessons, creating an art business with lithograph prints and designing porcelain collector plates. My prints were featured in national mail-order catalogs and from there I opened two art galleries to display my work.

During my 30s I had several readings from a well-known British medium, who encouraged me to develop my psychic gifts. He shared that my mind was capable of seeing and hearing information from the "spirit people," as he called them. Then, later while doing an art show, I saw my first vision of symbols. A female stranger was paying cash for a piece of my artwork and I saw initials floating above her head. When I asked her name, she confirmed that the initials correlated with her name! From then on I could actually see symbols in the auric field of other people, and the symbols always meant something to them. For example, one day when I was shopping at a local mall, I saw the image of a small rainbow hovering above a woman's head. It took courage to ask a stranger if that symbol meant anything, but indeed it did! She shared that her mother had recently passed away and on the day of her mother's funeral there was a bright rainbow over the cemetery. So it turned out that the *rainbow* was a spiritual connection between her mother and herself.

At the age of 40 I also saw my first departed human soul at a metaphysical conference. A lovely lady wanted me to *see* what impressions were in her auric field. As I looked up, there was a gentleman standing next to her, but not in physical form, because he appeared translucent. He telepathically gave me his name as John, and held up four fingers. I rapidly relayed to her what I was seeing. Indeed this was her grandfather and the lady had four daughters (which were his great granddaughters) that John telepathically described to me in detail. That incident, which was 25 years ago, started my psychic mediumship career.

I feel the first part of my life as an artist has enabled me to now vividly *see* the spirit world. Since then I've dedicated my time and energy to being a good medium, helping to bring comfort and healing to those grieving from the loss of loved ones. Over the years I've done thousands of phone readings, in-person readings, family group sessions and hundreds of spirit communication seminars. I have also enjoyed hosting my own radio and TV shows and have made numerous appearances on Fox, Comcast and ABC-TV. At present, I'm grateful to be on two major drive-time radio shows in Central PA. People call-in to receive readings and it's rewarding for me to help them. I must add that I believe in the power of prayer and God's protection which led me to become an ordained minister.

Although souls have communicated through me for years, I never asked them, nor did any of my clients ask them, "What are you doing in Heaven? What is it like to die and to make transition?" Because of this, I myself was very curious about what Heaven is like, and excited to start this book. This project *chose me*, and it just may give us a glimpse into the great unknown.

There is a tranquil sunroom in the back of our home, and other spiritual healers have told me that it is situated on a "lay-line of energy." This lay-line of energy has been described as a portal for souls to travel and communicate through. Indeed we have a private "peaceable kingdom" in our backyard, with a lot of land, trees, animals and birds.

To receive the information included in this book I would sit in our sunroom, meditate first and then pray for protection. Across from me was an empty chair, where departed souls would come to sit and telepathically converse. With a pen and paper in hand, I would rapidly jot down their communiqués using "automatic writing."[1] One by one, souls started appearing to convey how they perceived Heaven. My departed family members, clients and even people whom I had never met here on earth started sharing information. There was a realization that many souls shared common truths. Spirits described the levels of Heaven, the connecting portal of energy between worlds and the "book of life review." "Viewing stations" where souls can still see us on earth and the celestial temples of wisdom and learning were discussed. Others mentioned their individual "soul groups," being able to create a pleasant environment with their thought forms, choosing specific soul lessons before birth and reincarnation. I need to note that some of the souls used the words "light bodies," "spirits," "energy currents" and "beings" to describe themselves and others who they encountered in the next realm.

During my seminars, one of the first questions asked is, "Where is Heaven?" The distant universe that we perceive from earth is dark and this confuses people. "Where is the *light*, where does it exist?" they ask. Heaven is invisible to our physical world, yet it is a higher frequency, just as radio and TV waves have different

---

[1]Automatic writing is the process of writing material that does not come from the conscious thoughts of the writer.

frequencies! You can't see the television or hear the radio unless you have an instrument to tune into their signals. The same concept exists with communicating with the other side. Heaven's frequency surrounds the physical earth, but it takes a good medium to be the instrument to hear, see and feel the spirits from that realm.

I have also learned from the spirit world that mirrors are conduits for souls to travel through. We in the physical world are reflected in the front of the mirror, which creates our three-dimensional world. The back of the mirror is a neutral and solid plane, becoming a portal for souls to enter earth from the fourth dimension.

While conversing, I realized that each soul retained its own personality, mind, memory bank and consciousness. Therefore I kept these conversations in their purest form, without significantly editing information. I have changed or deleted some names for privacy reasons.

And as each individual perceives and describes things they encounter in the physical world in their own unique way, so do spirits describe their concept of Heaven from their own perspective. Also understand that these souls are trying to describe their spiritual experiences in physical terms that we can understand. As a result, some of the descriptions may at first seem contradictory.

There are certain concepts contained in this book that may be controversial. Many of these ideas are new to me, but I have chosen to keep them in the original form that they were given. One of these is the notion of incarnating back in time. From a scientific standpoint, the concept of paradox would seem to imply that this is not plausible. There are also several viewpoints that may be challenged by religious beliefs.

But with that said, I personally believe in a higher power called God. I believe that the spirit of God is within each of us, and that when we are freed from the physical shackles of our bodies, we are pure light bodies. We then, as souls, can join the Universal Mind that is God and become co-creators with that pure, unconditional love from whence we have come and shall always return.

I hope this book gives you a thought-provoking perspective of what you may experience in the soul place.

Love and blessings,

Michele A. Livingston

I believe that when death closes our eyes we shall
awaken to a light of which our sunlight
is but a shadow.

—Arthur Schopenhauer

1

Dorothy's Soul Place

My mother, Dorothy, was in her mid-40s when she fell in love and married my father, who was a confirmed bachelor at age 50. She was told that she could not have a child because the doctors discovered a huge fibroid tumor in her uterus. As opposed to what anyone thought or said, I was conceived and grew around the tumor in her abdomen. When I was delivered in 1951, I was called a "miracle child." After being enmeshed in the tumor, I was underweight and was born with a club foot and a curved spine. It took 18 hours for the doctors to deliver me! I almost died several times shortly after birth and up until the age of three. My mother and I were always very close spiritually and empathically. Dorothy later became an understanding mentor and best friend.

One morning, after praying and meditating in the sunroom I looked up and sitting in the "spirit chair" was my mother, Dorothy. She projected in a bright yellow color, imbued with golden radiance. Then she shared an account of her experiences in the soul place. The following is what Dorothy relayed:

The soul place where I reside is filled with light and magnificent colors one doesn't perceive on earth. "Sunbows" radiate everywhere with vibrating colors of the spectrum. The violet shades are intense, the cobalt blues glisten and the fuchsia pinks and golden yellows illuminate everything. I mention colors to you because you are an artist first and foremost. The love of art is where your talent was recognized, and that is what makes you a good visionary.

The Portal

There is a connecting portal between dimensions that spirals in a circular form. The portal walls (to some souls) can appear indigo blue with thousands of iridescent sparkles like glistening stars. To others it may appear like bright, blinding white light with bursts of color, like fireworks. My tunnel was glowing with amethyst purple light, which seemed to envelop me. You see, as every human being on earth perceives their own life's journey in a unique way, they also perceive their connecting portal in the way they think it should appear. As far as I know, none see it as a black hole, because they are headed towards the light of God.

God is pure unconditional love. It is love which created all, love which inspires good deeds, love which heals and renews and love which gives birth to all. When you see spirits in your readings, Michele, you see them as they want to project. Our light bodies are comprised of electromagnetic energy and thought forms. We use our thought forms to create a projection of how we want to appear. Today I wanted to project with golden light emanating from me, like an auric halo. When you have a drab gray day on earth, think of this golden light . . . and it will raise your spirit!

Transition

When I first made transition to this side, I was very tired and weak. Although I shed my physical body, my mind was exhausted and drained from trying to hang on to my earthly life. Even though we have "soul contracted" a timeline, one of the hardest things our "light body" does is to let go of the physical body. We can believe in God and Heaven, but we still don't know exactly what to expect. In the Christian religion we are taught about Heaven and Hell. Heaven is above and Hell is below.

Heaven is peace and eternal rest; Hell is fire, brimstone and damnation. And even though I was a devout Christian with a deep faith, I personally have not heard about or been aware of a fiery Hell. After our light body leaves the physical body, we are totally free; but we can still hear, see and feel in a spiritual sense. Our souls are capable of looking down at our lifeless bodies left behind before we start the "ascension." The ascension to this soul place means the soul travels upwards to the higher frequency.

The Reunion

After leaving the connecting portal, I first saw the Christ! We can also see departed loved ones coming for us, those we hold most dear, whoever they may be. Friends, relatives and even pets join us. We are embraced by them, and we are simply told, "Welcome home!" Our souls can meld with their souls and feel the pure love they give; we can feel their hugs and kisses, even though we no longer have our physical bodies. After entering Heaven, I was met by my dear mother, Leah, who passed away from influenza when I was only 12. I knew she would be waiting for me, and our spirits embraced! One tangible thing that I would like to clarify and that is easily accomplished here is the "melding of energy," which is feeling the other person's soul. You don't blend as one total being, but you can feel their love for you when you meld together. So to reunite is more than just *seeing* your loved ones; it's *feeling* them too. My mother Leah (your maternal grandmother) looked lovely and appeared around the age of 30. As I have stated, light bodies can project the way they want to appear. Most female spirits choose to look like they did in their favorite time of life, when they were happy, healthy and radiant. A male spirit may choose to project strong, virile and handsome.

The essence of the soul is electro-magnetic energy, which is androgynous or sexless. When I refer to souls *projecting* to you, I'm using examples of how we remember them as being male or female while they were living on earth.

In regards to children, I would like to briefly discuss the formative years. Children who passed at a young age may project young, so they are recognized when their parents join them. But indeed, some of the children are old souls who have had many incarnations. Children in the formative years, from one to five, are still connected to this dimension and can see spirits. When a soul enters a baby body, there is an abrupt transition, and that is why babies sleep a lot. The infants are adjusting to the denser, lower frequency of the earth plane. Remember that children can see spirits and the members of their own soul group. The formative years are known as the alpha state. When children start elementary school, most gradually enter into the beta state, where they intuitively block this invisible world. To forget this higher realm enables children to learn and grow without the distractions of the spirit world.

I want to add that when we look at you on earth from this realm of light, we do not see you physically, but we perceive your heart light and your auric field (which is the light that surrounds you).

After we recognize and greet our departed loved ones, they bid us to come with them for a homecoming "reunion." With their collective thought forms, a familiar place will be created for you. If you enjoyed the outdoors, an open green meadow may be formulated where you will initially feel comfortable. The area created could even be your grandmother's kitchen if fond memories still linger there. There is no time here, so the reunion may last several minutes or years in earthly terms. Time, as we know it, is man-made on earth to keep a semblance of order. In fact, those humans living on earth are the only creatures that deal with time!

Soul Groups

The next step is meeting up with your individual "soul group" in this dimension, which can be comprised of up to 5000 or more souls! These are souls you love and who love you. These light bodies have had many earthly incarnations with you, and some are "spirit guides" of yours. Spirit guides can be deceased relatives that you knew from your present incarnation on earth, or can be from past lives that you have experienced together. When you see these spirits again, you know them—even if you had forgotten who they were after you incarnated on earth. Of course when you were born there was a form of amnesia your soul experienced when entering a new physical body.

The Life Review

After communing with your vast soul group, it is time for your life review. There are some who think that they are going to be judged by an angry God, sitting on a throne. But the energy of God is pure love and light, which does not condemn us. Therefore we objectively judge ourselves. An area is telepathically created for your life review by your guides' collective thought forms. It appears like a huge hologram or three-dimensional movie. Here you will observe your first to your last breath. Then you will simultaneously see, feel and hear every action, thought and intention during the course of your lifetime. Nothing is hidden in your life review. Those people who you genuinely loved and felt compassion for will be shown and you will feel their happiness. Conversely those you have hurt, abused or ignored will also be viewed, and you will feel and see their emotional distress. This process is merely an objective review, and not a criticism of your thoughts and actions.

When this procedure is completed you are taken to your specific "Council of Light." Your council may be comprised of your spirit guides and also angels (who are light beings) since not all in your council are necessarily human souls. These beings may appear standing or sitting around a large table. Whatever your created environment may be, though, it is always surrounded by bright white light. The council beings may wear white robes, and sometimes golden light emanates from them, creating beautiful auras. They will ask you various questions such as, "How do you think your soul progressed in your last life? What motivations inspired your actions? Did you fulfill your soul contracted mission? Were your pre-chosen soul lessons learned? How did you love?"

In essence each life is about the love you give, the interactions you have and the soul tasks that are accomplished. It's that simple! Your personal life review pertains to individuals you have known in your last incarnation. It may be deemed admirable during a lifetime to start large foundations for others welfare, or become involved in great causes. But your review will show a daily snapshot of who you are, moment by moment, with the people who surround you and how you have touched each individual.

If, for example, you're waiting in the checkout line at the grocery store and the person behind you is in a hurry with a screaming child, you may spontaneously let them go ahead of you. That act is one of courtesy, or as you say on earth, a "random act of kindness." Conversely, if you dangerously cut in front of another vehicle and curse at the other driver, this also will be viewed and understood. These random situations are not premeditated for you to be good and kind; they just happen during your lifetime. In summation, your life review is about your day-to-day journey and not the total culmination of your life.

The Gray Area

As I have stated, I am so far not aware of a fire and brimstone Hell, but I have heard of a place called the "gray area." As there are different frequencies in this dimension, I am aware of a lower stratum, close to the dense heavy energy of earth. It appears foggy and gray in color. Some spirits will enter this area for a while until they are *aware* of the higher level of light and are ready for their life review. These are souls who have physically lived in darkness, negativity, greed or anger while on earth. Thus this region may consist of murderers, rapists, abusers and those who commit heinous crimes.

All souls are from the Godhead and were created in love. But the gifts of free choice and free will were bestowed upon humankind; therefore some have strayed from goodness and love. I have heard that this lower, denser place feels barren, dreary and desolate. Spirits may wander aimlessly through this area, or they may be in a sleep state. Human spirit guides and angels of light go down to that level and try to coax these spirits to come up to this frequency for their life reviews. While on earth they may have lived in fear and confusion, so many times they refuse assistance. The gray area houses spirits who have forgotten about forgiveness, compassion and love.

So a spirit like Hitler, who was driven by power and ego, resulting in the death of thousands of people, would inhabit the gray area. There are also cases of human souls who are involved in violent crimes before they die and can become a little disoriented and confused upon arrival here. There is no time here, so lost souls can stay in this condition for thousands of earth years. When they finally awaken to the truth and understand where they are, they will hopefully agree to their life review. It takes effort and determination on the part of advanced soul volunteers to go down and try to help lost souls get to their life review. The soul volunteers who travel to the gray area are essentially "heroes," for this is a difficult task.

Reincarnation

Several days later I had another meeting with my mother, Dorothy. This time she sat across from me bathed in rose pink light from head to toe. Dorothy said:

I would like to share what I've learned about reincarnation. In a strange analogy (one that you never thought I would give), think of the egg in a woman's womb representing the Creator. The sperm represent souls trying to reach the egg to become one, once again, with the Godhead. This process is the evolutionary journey of all souls—to reincarnate again and again, returning home to the Creative Source, which is God.

The core of creation encompasses this concept of the soul's return and is played out over and over with each lifetime. During a lifetime, the chosen subject of an individual soul's mission could be geared to healing, teaching, creating or even inventing. The chosen virtues to be learned could be patience, tolerance or humility. But the crux of each lesson goes back to love, which is how we have treated our fellow humans. Self-love must also be recognized and enacted upon. Many times we are not taught how to love ourselves, only others. Remember, you are one with the love of Universal Knowledge. As you are aware of loving others, also be aware of loving self. Many people neglect their own welfare. The Spirit of God is within all and through all that exists; therefore to honor God, you must remember to honor self.

Just for a moment, think of traveling throughout the world that you now live in. There are numerous places, both great and small, to view and visit—from the grandeur of canyons, mountains and seas to the intimacy of the smallest neighborhood town. Similarly there are many cultures, races, religions and traditions that you will never see or learn about in a single lifetime. Trying to grasp the concept of traveling throughout your world, visiting every single place and getting to know every individual can be mind boggling. The ability to do this could not be accomplished during one's lifetime, or even thousands of lifetimes for that matter.

If you would choose to travel back and visit the civilizations of ancient Greece or Egypt to learn about their arts, music and culture, it would again take thousands of lifetimes. So to think about actually experiencing all that has been and will be on the earth plane is an overwhelming scenario to grasp.

Certain light bodies (or souls) are constantly reincarnating on earth. They may soul contract to incarnate in a physical body as early Neanderthal man and chronologically continue through the evolutionary process every century!

Yet not all souls have the same desire to experience the physical world. Some prefer to study and learn about various cultures without actually incarnating into them. In this realm there are vast spiritual libraries and universities where every civilization and aspect of human society can be studied. To study here though is not as in-depth or profound as learning to cope in a physical body while in a physical world.

In this present dissertation I will not cover life on other planets, star belts or parallel universes, although life does exist throughout the cosmos. There is more than enough to study while living on the earth plane for many millennia. Souls upon returning to Heaven (the "true home") remember all of their incarnations, remember their soul group and their guides. The composition of a soul is androgynous or sexless energy, but it can choose to enter either a male or female body to carry out various soul lessons.

There are some people who have lived in darkness for a long time on earth—maybe their entire lives. By "darkness" I mean they have lived in a void of extreme negativity. Therefore some souls do not immediately *remember* the love of Heaven after they pass on. We know that all spirits who are born on earth come from a state of purity and love. But we also need to consider what happens to these physical human beings after they take their first breath and address the thousands of choices that they will make during their lifetime. Their accumulated choices enable them to either have a smooth transition, or be in a darkened state of denial when they arrive on this side. The concept of making choices is not all about consciously being good or bad during a lifetime. The truth of this concept is about a person's spontaneous intentions on a daily basis and the actions exhibited to not only themselves but to others.

For example, when a light body chooses to be born in the ghetto, it knows before entering the baby body how much adversity there will be. In choosing that environment, there may be more of a predisposition for violence, substance abuse, poverty, intimidation and lack of education. Therefore a soul may choose to incarnate in the ghetto to learn courage, be aware of self discipline or to overcome obstacles and forgive others. This living condition may also help an individual to learn to love self and hasten spiritual progression. To reiterate, younger souls have had fewer incarnations and tend to be more selfish and narrow minded. Older souls have had many earthly incarnations, and by doing so have learned kindness and compassion. So in the ranks of society, if a human being chooses to live in squalor, it does not necessarily mean that person's soul is a young soul. The same is true for an individual who is uneducated or destitute. Conversely a highly educated, well bred, wealthy and charming individual may still be a young soul. A person's intentions and actions mirror their soul's level of development.

The Issue of Killing

If an individual kills another person to gain material wealth, that is coined greed. If a person murders another to be with their spouse or lover, that is termed lust. And if someone takes another's life just for revenge, that is deemed anger. On the other hand, if a person kills in self defense or to save another's life, to protect another family member, or even during military service, the *motive* behind the act is different. The act then becomes one of protection, courage or valor rather than greed, lust or anger. Therefore not all people's souls who take another's life go to a lower darker frequency. But it does seem that those souls whose actions were purely self-centered may at first reside in the gray area.

The act of taking another's life is not "cut and dry" as you say on earth. Those who take another's life for good intentions may come immediately into our frequency of light. Others whose motivations are selfish need time to awaken to the truth, understand their own intentions and be responsible for their actions. Each human soul will always be given another chance to awaken and to love, for we all are from the goodness and light of the Godhead, and we will always eventually return to that inner sanctum.

A few days later, I once again longed to hear from my mother. But I know in Heaven, souls have their own spiritual agenda. We, as mediums, are not capable of conjuring up the departed, nor hopefully would we want to. The departed will communicate when they are ready. After a couple of weeks had passed, I was eating breakfast at the kitchen table, and I glanced out into our adjoining sunroom. There, sitting in the spirit chair was my beautiful mother, Dorothy. For this visit she projected in pale blue chiffon and wore silver shoes covered in crystals! My mother continued:

Teachers

I enjoy teaching other souls here, and with my thought forms I have created a "Grand Hall of Learning." I always loved France (because of my many incarnations there) and so my hall of learning is similar to the "Hall of Mirrors" in the Palace of Versailles. My created space is long and rather narrow, but many souls can gather there. I appeared to you today dressed in my earthly clothes, but when I teach in this realm I project in silk chiffon flowing robes, which glow with iridescent sunbow colors. As you know, I was an English teacher while on earth, and I enjoyed enlightening others. In this realm I do not need to teach language, because there is just one "universal language." But I teach newly arrived souls who have been physically or emotionally hurt while on earth to forgive their perpetrators. Even though they have shed their physical bodies, a few light bodies still carry animosity. After their life review, they can come to me, if they wish, to learn about love and compassion. I try to encourage them to release guilt or other negative residual emotions. Since I passed away in 1993, I have chosen to teach. There is no time here, so the length of each class I conduct could be a year or more in your earth time. I only enlighten souls for one class. Then new souls can sign up. On this side we are never forced to do anything, but gratefully many new arrivals choose to learn about empathy from me.

In this realm I have also chosen to teach souls about kindness and mercy. These virtues are the core of all that is good. I want to address teaching, because teachers are so valued on this side; they enable other souls to spiritually progress. Teachers are the ones who have had many incarnations and various life experiences—some pleasant and some tragic. Through these varied experiences while on earth, they have learned many virtues, some of which are patience, humility, compassion, tolerance and unconditional love. Even the appreciation of music, color theory, the arts and design concepts have been honed in this dimension.

We consider soul progression like the levels of school. You have probably encountered extremely young souls inhabiting a human body who are self-centered and egotistical. On a spiritual school level they would be in kindergarten. Kindergarten is a German word which means "children's garden." All souls are infinite beings, yet learning about the trials of the physical world is important for understanding soul evolution. Some souls may choose to progress only in this realm, but by doing so they will not experience physical and emotional dilemmas. To choose the crash course of physical birth takes courage and advances the soul more rapidly. Souls who have only briefly inhabited human bodies have not had the in-depth life experiences to grow spiritually. They see the world as a playground for themselves; they want their own needs met and do not question anything. If they have any belief systems, they possibly have been taught those beliefs from parents and others, which is fine. Again, this is merely an observation of them and not a criticism on my part.

It may take younger souls many lifetimes to graduate to a spiritual first grade, so to speak. With each grade of spiritual development, the soul has learned many lessons through various incarnations. Therefore, spirit teachers in this realm would be considered as advanced college professors. They are more progressed because while in physical form they have learned many crucial lessons through trials and tribulations. And even in between earthly lifetimes, teachers have spiritually advanced by studying at temples of wisdom and learning. It takes determination to incarnate again and again, knowing beforehand all of the hard tasks you have soul contracted to learn. At this very moment, people who are now living on earth are still proceeding (at their own pace) and have not yet reached the spiritual PhD level. Once you reach the highest level of pure compassion, earthly incarnations are no longer necessary. An ascended master and teacher like Jesus has fully understood the concept of unconditional love, and many souls study and learn from Him here.

On this side there are also "levels" which are frequencies of light. Younger souls, who were filled with greed, hungry for power and driven by ego, would go to the lower gray level. This would equate to nursery school on earth. In this lower stratum, there are rehabilitation stations where a light body can be awakened and remember unconditional love. Because there is no space here, these rehab stations are created by the thought forms of advanced souls, who are called the "collective consciousness."

Older, more advanced souls can become volunteers who agree to awaken and teach younger souls. A small percentage of younger souls may even sleep in the lower frequency because they are self absorbed, confused and in denial. All of us were created in pure love, but because of God's gift of free choice, some have strayed from the truth. The spiritual truth is that we are all one, we are all equal and we were all created in love as light bodies before physical bodies were conceived. When a soul incarnates into a physical body on earth and is reminded of that truth, he or she no longer carries the heavy baggage of negativity from the past. Any human being can overcome tragedy, loss, abuse or degradation by first being aware of the pain, releasing it, forgiving the perpetrators and moving on through love. But this concept is easier said than done while living on the earth plane!

Teachers on this side can choose any innovative subject to help enlighten others. A teaching subject can range from composing musical notes into master compositions to designing and producing beautiful artwork to creative writing for self-expression. We don't talk, but send information to each other's minds through telepathy. Temples of learning are available to study subjects such as science, human evolution and even how to use original ideas for future inventions. Souls who have studied certain subjects may then choose to become spiritual mentors for those humans on earth who are interested in these subjects. Sometimes a person on earth will say, "That idea came out of the blue!" Indeed, creative ideas on any subject are often inspired by spirit teachers on this side.

Crystal City

On a warm summer's day, I was relaxing on our upper deck. The deck is located directly above the sunroom where I normally conduct spirit conversations. The energy is peaceful there because it is situated on our land's diagonal "lay line of energy" that runs through our home. This area is indeed like a portal for spirits, and communication with the other side is as clear on the deck as it is in the sunroom below. It was a gorgeous afternoon and I was not only able to see over the trees, but down into the valley. The sky was aqua blue and a gentle warm breeze enveloped me. My mother Dorothy appeared this time wearing a bright fuchsia suit with a circular lapel pin. The pink, green and purple stones in the pin sparkled in the sunlight. She looked lovely, projecting in her early 40s (about the age when she gave birth to me). Dorothy smiled and was very happy to be with me. I telepathically asked her about creating environments and about the "Crystal City" that other people have described and seen during their near-death experiences (NDEs). She replied:

Environments can be created here with thought forms. So for example, an artist who wants to teach painting techniques may formulate a huge, glorious art studio. Or a well-known musician and composer may telepathically conjure an immense music hall where souls can actually become one with musical tones and frequencies. In this realm we are co-creators with the Godhead and all is good.

Of course in this higher light there is no room for pride, ego or competition. Souls should love what they do here for spiritual progression. And there is fun and laughter and merriment! Since there is no longer negativity, addictions, greed or lust, there is an abundance of peace, love, happiness and laughter. Merriment is good for the soul!

Certain spirits, just like people on earth, do not wish to immediately study or learn. My brother (your uncle Harold) has created a sparkling stream where his joy is catching fish! That was his passion on earth, and it's his passion here, for the time being.

There is a higher frequency of light which contains temples of wisdom, learning and teaching. Residing in these temples are some of the ascended master teachers. Some souls call this place the "City of Lights" or the Crystal City. The individual structures are immense and translucent. They glisten like cut crystal cathedrals and are of many shapes and sizes. A few have columns like the temples in Ancient Greece. And other architectural structures have high faceted spires, along with open air crystal pavilions. The energy of the Christ consciousness and the Buddha consciousness reside here for example. Residing in the Crystal City are also advanced teachers, saints and prophets.

So in summation, not all souls may experience the same situations that I have experienced in Heaven. I am merely sharing what I have learned so far on my spiritual journey in the soul place.

2

The Angelic Kingdom

During the course of these soul dialogues, angels were occasionally mentioned. To gain a greater perspective, I asked my own spirit guide, Daniel, about angels. Daniel said:

Angels have never been human souls. They are "light frequencies" which emanate from the energy of the Creator. They were created to oversee, guard and inspire the development of the human race. Angels are messengers and protectors of the human populace. They reside, not among human souls as spirit guides do, but have their origin in a much higher, faster frequency. Angels are assigned to individual human beings at birth, depending on what their soul is trying to learn for a specific lifetime. So guardian angels rotate for each individual's incarnation. Souls have nothing to learn from angels as angels have had no human life experiences on earth. But souls can commune with angels in Heaven if they wish. However the angelic frequency is so intensely higher that it's difficult for souls to sustain consistent communication with them. As a soul would store energy and lower frequency to talk through a medium on earth, so the soul must raise energy and frequency to commune with the Angelic Kingdom.

It is not difficult for angels to raise or lower their frequencies because they are pure light beings and do not have the denser energetic bodies as humans do. Therefore they can easily come down to earth to help us or go even higher into other dimensions of energy.

Angelic beings do not need to study, develop or learn lessons as they are not a part of our human condition. They can visit Heaven or earth if assigned to, but do not reside in either place. These light beings are not "ascended masters" either. Ascended masters are human souls who have reached their ascended status through many incarnations in which they have mastered all of the virtues. Some of the virtues mastered are patience, humility, wisdom, compassion and unconditional love. Humans can study with the ascended ones who reside in Heaven, but cannot study with the light beings known as angels.

Guardian angels can indeed meet us when we make transition to Heaven, because they are liaison messengers and greeters. When a human soul is then settled into Heaven, the guardian angels work is done and that light being goes back to the higher energy frequency of its own dimension.

When you see Heaven portrayed with angels sitting on clouds, that is just partly the case. Their true mission is an interim one for us, both on earth and in Heaven.

On one occasion I was relaxing on a balcony at a resort and surprisingly the soul of a priest came through to communicate. He was someone I had never met, but he wanted to talk about angels. He wore a robe with a white priest's collar and he gave me his name as Anthony. He also mentioned the different strata of Heaven and the Crystal City where some of the ascended masters reside. The following is priest Anthony's viewpoint on angels:

I am Anthony, and I was a priest in Italy during the last century. I was always curious about the saints and angels, especially the archangels—Michael, Gabriel and Raphael, who were my companions in my last lifetime. I had visionary powers similar to yours, Michele, and I communed with archangels, although I never disclosed these abilities to the clergy.

While on earth, when fear would descend upon me (as it does everyone at times), I would call upon my divine protector, which was Archangel Michael. I could see him clearly in my mind's eye. He projected as a very tall presence, sometimes wearing armor and holding a shield of protection and a sword of courage. We would converse frequently, and I would think of Joan of Arc who truly was a disciple of Archangel Michael. After a visionary appearance from Michael, I would always feel safe.

Archangel Gabriel seemed to be a more gentle being, one of wisdom and truth, and appeared as a divine messenger. If there was a problem with the clergy I would invoke Gabriel, with God's permission, for answers. And this communication would always bring closure and peace to the situation.

During personal health concerns, Archangel Raphael, the divine healer, would minister to me and give me insights about my health condition. I found great solace and comfort in communicating with the archangels, while always understanding that God was the Divine Creator and they were just emissaries of His light.

My heart failed me at the end of my life, and I transitioned quickly to the light. I first encountered Jesus wearing a snow white sparkling robe with His whole being emanating the brightest light. Master Jesus greeted me and embraced me with the purest feeling of unconditional love. That peaceful feeling flowed through my soul like warm honey. Immediately after that embrace, I looked for my companion friends, the archangels, but they did not appear. Nor did I see any of the saints, which confused me! Next, my earthly mother Anna greeted me and my father Joseph, followed by an entire heavenly family of aunts, uncles and siblings who had passed away before me. We had a family reunion, and it was wonderful.

I was inspired to learn that a couple of my human relatives were my spirit helpers. One was my paternal grandfather, and the other was my great aunt, my maternal grandmother's sister. This place of light was my true home, and I seemed to meld with the love of God. I telepathically asked those who greeted me, "Where are my angels?" The answer was always, "Later."

After encountering my panoramic past life review, I shared with my spirit helpers what I had learned from that lifetime. It felt good to know that I had learned the soul lessons that I agreed to learn, one of which was faith. "Did I want to now study or teach here in Heaven?" my spirit guides asked. "Not yet," I said, but I still wanted to know where the saints and angels reside.

Then a huge being of light appeared as a pulsating column. The radiant form then changed into a somewhat human looking being. I knew this being was an angel, because the energy was different from the other human souls that I had already encountered. The angel looked androgynous—neither male nor female—but projected a powerful, almost overwhelming presence. It telepathically sent me the following:

> Hark, I am an angelic being of God's light, and I come to answer your question. There are different strata or frequencies of Heaven. As your earth has different layers, so does this realm.
>
> There is a sub realm we refer to as the gray area. Here reside troubled souls who are lost, who do not believe in love or in God and have lived in darkness while on earth. Some are mass murderers, torturers or rapists and have caused much pain to other humans. They sleep or walk aimlessly and lifelessly in the gray mist. Volunteer human souls and sometimes assigned angels will go down to awaken them to the truth or coax them to come to the light. Many beings rejoice in Heaven when a soul in darkness is awakened and will

agree to come and experience their book of life (life review). Only then can these souls see the darkness of their ways and accept responsibility for the pain they have inflicted! They are rehabilitated by counselors of light and sent onward to remember and accept the love and light of God.

Next there is the realm where you are now, Anthony. This is where most souls initially come. Here you may create your own heaven with your thought forms because you are one with the love of God and a co-creator with God. You are a child of the Father/Mother God, made in that image. In this realm you have freedom to study, teach, create, volunteer or train to be a guide to help those on earth. There are as many things to do spiritually in Heaven as there are to do physically on earth.

Now the higher frequency realms are where the saints and ascended masters reside. They are evolved older souls of light and pure unconditional love. You may travel there to study with them and learn from the ascended ones. This area is where the Crystal City is located. Each ascended master inhabits a crystal room of light where they teach souls about love and the higher consciousness. The saints and ascended masters, like Christ, are housed in one huge crystal structure and each has his or her own large room. Jesus himself said, "My father's house has many rooms; if that were not so, would I have told you that I am going to prepare a place for you?"[1] This higher realm of learning is for souls who are serious seekers of the truth.

No human souls can enter the "angelic realm" which is the next higher level of frequency. Angels and the powerful archangels do exist, and they are beings of light who were created by God to assist humankind

[1] John 14:2

on their spiritual journey. But a human soul cannot enter that realm because the frequency is too high. Angels are androgynous beings, neither male nor female essence. They do not possess free choice or free will as human souls do. They merely carry out assignments to help, guide, protect, assist and are messengers to those on earth.

A guardian angel is assigned at birth to each individual. But guardian angels can change with each soul's new incarnation. If you would like to speak with an archangel or angel, you can invoke them, with God's will, to come down and meet with you (as you did, Anthony, while on earth). But you, as a human soul, will never be able to encounter or enter their extremely high frequency.

With that answer, this great being of light left my presence. I now understand that at any time, whether on earth or in this realm, I can call upon angels to guide me if it is the Creator's will as well. For now though I wish to visit and access the Crystal City to meet and learn from the saints and the ascended master, Jesus.

One summer day in 1991, a sweet young lady with platinum blonde hair came to receive a reading from me. I had just opened my second art gallery, displaying my artwork in the large front room. In the back office I was doing consultations and recording them on an accompanying tape player. The lady seemed to love her reading and she sent me a lovely thank you note. Her name was Candy. After her reading, Candy left her place of employment to pursue her spiritual journey. She traveled across the country to study and learn about angels, for that was her calling. She also became very involved in organizing metaphysical expos along with presenting her findings at our local metaphysical bookstore.

I was sad to learn that she developed an aggressive form of breast cancer, and Candy passed away in 2014. Only a few days after she passed, I was in the sunroom to see what spirit would like to communicate. To my delight it was Candy! She sat in the spirit chair across from me and looked like an angel herself, projecting in a pale aqua suit. Then she telepathically started to communicate:

Hi Michele, I wish you well. I prided myself on being an "angel expert," and I will soon find out all about them. As you know, I passed only a few days ago. My personal life was always in turmoil; my spiritual life grounded me. I enjoyed helping people to "awaken" as you call it and helping them to get in touch with their own spirituality.

There are many things I wanted to do like write a book —but I just didn't lean that way. There are only so many things to do in a lifetime. My husband and son will miss me, of course, along with some friends, but life goes on. I was very tired and ready to go. I really wasn't afraid, as I counted on angels being there.

Angels are emissaries or as you call them light beings. They are powerful, but they do not heal, only enact upon what they are told to do by God. So when you say that you are sending "healing angels" to someone, in reality you mean you are sending healing energy.

Yes, I thought I was the proverbial angel expert, but as yet I have only encountered one—and that is my guardian angel helper. He is very tall and protective. I saw him when I left my body, and he appeared as an orb of bright golden light. In the center of that huge aura of light was the form of a being. That being I recognized as my guardian angel.

It seems I have one foot on earth and one in Heaven right now. I will be attending my own memorial service coming up, and of course haven't gone through my book of life review as yet. I wanted you to know that I will return to talk to you at a later date. Although I can't give you lots of information on the angelic kingdom now, I will in the future. I count you as a good and accurate medium, and I would like you to include me in your book on Heaven.

Angels play a huge role in this world of the beyond. I want to contribute by telling you all I know and will learn about them. You're correct in saying angels vibrate with certain colors. Angels will typically take on an androgynous form and then emanate a color. I know many times you see them as "columns of light," but I saw my guardian angel so far as a human looking male form with golden light around him.

Angels with a purple hue bring insight, intuition and psychic wisdom. An angel with a surrounding indigo or royal blue color designates communication, calm and protection. An emerald green angelic aura represents nature and healing. Although angels themselves cannot heal, they can bring a flow of healing energy from God to a person on earth.

To me, aqua is the most beautiful light and my favorite color (that's why I'm projecting wearing an aqua suit). But my own guardian angel protects me with bright golden yellow light representing balance and clarity. Next an orange hue denotes creativity and inspiration and a bright, ruby red light that surrounds an angel, represents passion and vitality.

All this I know right now, but there will be much more to learn in the days ahead. I chose to come to you now because I know that you will include my angel information in your book. I will return to tell you more. Thanks for listening.

About six months later I was again in the sunroom praying and when I opened my eyes and glanced up, the "angel lady" was there once more! Candy sat across from me projecting with pale blonde hair, wearing a diaphanous sparkling white gown, silver shoes and surrounded by a rose pink auric glow. She continued with her dialogue:

Hi Michele, Happy New Year. I know you're sitting down to hear messages from your clients who have passed away, but first I want to share what the angelic kingdom is like. When you did a reading for me over 20 years ago, I was working at a bank and had just given birth to my one and only son. You *awakened* me to my spiritual journey, and I knew then that I had to press on for a higher cause. I left the workaday world and became an entrepreneur, traveling the country, healing and enlightening people. I enjoyed teaching Reiki and alternative ways of healing, but my main mission was sharing information about angels.

You are correct in saying that angels are androgynous (sexless) and have never been human souls. They are liaisons and assistants of the Creator. They take assignments to help and protect those on earth. Everyone is born with an assigned guardian angel. That angel is with them always until the end of their life on earth. Angels do not have free choice as we humans have, but they are on a designated schedule to help keep a person on track with his or her soul mission.

I enjoyed my work with the angelic energy and when I contracted breast cancer, I was determined to stay on earth for as long as possible! Life is beautiful and there was a lot to be thankful for. I've only been in Heaven a few months as you know. Every soul meets with his or her own individual council, some of which are spirit guides (human souls) and others are angels (light beings). My spirit council is comprised of 12 beings, three of which are angels. The angels' names are Azael, Doriel, and Sharele. You're correct in saying that the letters "EL" create a higher vibration for a name. Those letters in the Hebrew translation mean "like unto God." I have learned that about 90% of angelic names here have an "EL" contained in them.

I would like to study directly with the angels and archangels, but it has been forbidden. The angels are emissaries of God and were created in perfection to serve humanity. They reside in a very high energy frequency. We as human souls are pure light, but from a spiritual perspective, when we inhabit a human body, we become imperfect. Even though the soul does have the capacity to direct the mind and influence the physical body, we are still tempted in many ways and can lose our self-control on earth. Negative emotions can lead to anger, greed and the craving for power. So in Heaven we must learn from more advanced human souls about what purpose our mission served, and not learn from the angels. The angelic kingdom has no frame of reference for our earthly lives because they have never been human.

Angels and archangels are powerful beings and are a collective consciousness of the highest order. We can call upon them to help us while on earth, but only God can give angels the "green light" to come down and help us.

On earth the most common pleas that we have for angels are for healing, protection and guidance. It is true that we can only *see* angels when they occasionally take human form in our times of need.

I loved to teach about angels while on earth, and I assumed I could study with them. Now I realize that the ones to study with for soul progression are ascended human souls. So for now, that is what I plan to do in Heaven.

Blessings and light,
Candy

3

Welcoming New Arrivals

I was in my kitchen brewing a cup of hot tea with my mind in neutral, and that's when I heard a familiar voice say, "Hi, it's Cousin Mary." Mary had been married to my dad's cousin, Richard, who was very well-to-do as the owner of a large shoe factory in the 1940s. She was widowed at a fairly young age, never had children and never remarried. When I asked Cousin Mary why she never remarried, she replied with her droll sense of humor, "I could never find another handsome man with money who would keep the toilet seat down!"

Mary collected exquisite antiques and not only had a rich history of knowing opera but had the opportunity to visit some of the finest opera houses. Mary's uncle, John Luther Long, wrote the original story entitled Madame Butterfly. Long's story became a one act play that premiered in New York in 1900. Later, the play Madame Butterfly moved to London where Puccini saw it and was inspired to create the famous opera from the original story.

Cousin Mary traveled the world, and I was excited to receive postcards from every port she visited. She had a long joyful life, I feel, in part due to her love of people. At age 85 she was delivering "Meals on Wheels" to the "old people," as she called them (some much younger than she). Mary peacefully passed away at the age of 104! The following was her communiqué:

I'm fascinated with your book about the afterlife, as nobody really knows what to expect. But I want to first thank you for being kind to me, visiting me to the very end of my life. It's a wonderful world in this soul place, and as you say, a higher, faster frequency. We do retain all of our memories; our minds are sharp, and there is no pain. We communicate through sheer telepathy by sending thoughts and images to each other.

In my opinion it's important, while living on earth, to honor the elderly. In many ancient cultures the elders were revered and honored, but not so in today's society. I have made new friends here and have met up with some of my old ones. We have formed a soul group for a common cause. Most of us in our soul group lived to be in the mid-90s to well over 100 years of age. Our "cause" is to help those people cross over who lived a long rich life but were alone at the end. On earth, some elderly people are scared, some feel forgotten or forsaken and some no longer have a family and are lonely or disheartened. A few of them, when they make transition, are just a little confused. Those who had dementia may also be slightly disoriented when they pass away. I want to clarify that not all souls who had these physical conditions are confused upon arrival, just a small percentage.

Here we call the group that we have formed the "Welcome Committee," which you will probably find amusing. Our original committee consisted of about 1000 souls, but now others want to join in. When distraught spirits, such as those mentioned, look for their loved ones, they may have a hard time visualizing them at first. We're there to greet the new arrivals with love and patience. At times we splinter off from each other and form new committee groups. Remember, there is no time or space here, so it's our *energy* and *intent* that helps those in need. We telepathically talk to them and tell them that they have made transition and not to be afraid. Eventually their minds become more lucid and they *remember* where they are—their true home! Then when their family reunion starts we step away.

I have also reconnected with my uncle John, who wrote the original Madame Butterfly story. We still can visit Victorian opera halls, if we wish, that are created with our thought forms. That is quite a pleasure of mine. And my dear husband Richard, who is my true soul mate, is always here for me. This place truly is Heaven—the place we call home.

When I was growing up I remember that my mother's older brother, Harold was one of the kindest men I had ever known. He always had a thick head of hair, and in his later years his hair turned snow white. My mother, Dorothy, and my uncle were best friends, and both of them remained very close to the end of their lives. Harold was always joyful and full of life. It was obvious he loved people. His favorite sport was fishing, and he prided himself on not only catching large fish, but providing many meals for our family.

A couple of months after my uncle passed away, I had a lucid dream of him. Only his face and shoulders appeared to me. At first he was wearing a military hat that changed into several different looking hats. The last one he wore was a pointed straw hat with a chin band. It looked like a conical sun hat that Chinese wear when working in rice paddies. Uncle Harold telepathically sent me the thought that now he was one of my spirit guides. He also added that the different hats represented the past life times we shared together.

It is known that if you can remember a lucid dream many years later, the dream is then called a vision. The vision of him occurred in 1990. I was ecstatic that one of the last souls to communicate with me before the book went to press was my dear uncle. Harold said to me:

What'cha doin' honey? It's your uncle Harold. I came by to say hello and say that we are very proud of you in Heaven. Your mother and I are still together at times and have had some good chats.

You know I loved to fish, so I have created a park area with a large lake where I go fishing. I'm from your soul group in Heaven, and we have had past lives together.

When I lived on earth I never thought about past lives, but indeed I know about them now.

Upon arrival in Heaven we are met by guides and relatives that we remember. Then we can go our separate ways if we wish. Along with the enjoyment of nature and fishing, I personally like to welcome and organize things for souls who have recently made transition. A few may enter here a little confused and don't know where they are. I lend them my energy to direct them as to where to go and what to do. I loved to help people on earth, and enjoy guiding "new arrivals" here until they are squared away.

This place we call Heaven is not complicated like earth can be. It's simple—without struggle, disease or negativity. People aren't used to a perfect world at first, because the earth is a training ground. There are things we all need to learn when we live on earth to help our soul's progression. When new arrivals realize that the light in Heaven is perfect, they are sometimes in disbelief! I can help them *remember* that it was *here* that their souls were created, and that here they have returned to the "perfect light."

Everyone loves this realm because we are not forced or pushed to do anything. So I've kept it simple for myself. I go fishing and meditate while doing so. I welcome, direct and counsel new arrivals. This is a wonderful world filled with joy and beauty.

As you know your mother and I were very close on earth, and over here we still have that same closeness.

Sending love and happiness to you always,
Uncle Harold

4

Creating Environments

It was about 1981 when I first heard of a renowned British medium from Yorkshire, England named Don. I learned that he was a leading figure in the Spiritualist Movement, and that earned him the title of the "Archbishop of Spiritualism." He was visiting our area, here in Central Pennsylvania, to do consultations. I immediately contacted the person he was staying with and booked a reading. I had never had a reading with a medium and didn't have a clue as to what to expect. I was told to bring along a small tape recorder and tape, or to have a notebook and pen in hand. My heart was racing when I arrived for our appointment. The charming gentleman I met was just that—a refined, intelligent person who was the founder of the Lynnwood Fellowship in the UK. He shared that he was also a teacher and author.

In a dimly lit room the reading began. I was sitting across from Don when he started communicating with my father, who passed away in 1966 from brain cancer. Details were shared that no one else knew. I was so happy and relieved to know that my father's spirit saw my development. He was at my graduation, both from high school and college, and watched my progression through life.

When Don visited again, I had my second consultation with him. It was at this session that the future of my mediumship abilities was mentioned! Seeds were planted in my mind to entertain the thought of communicating with spirits. My mind, he said, was so channeled as to perceive of the spirit world—their thoughts, their ways and intentions. Yes, the "spirit people" (as he called them) wanted to work with me. It was as if permission was given to me to pursue this career. However, Don warned me that this energy work was exhausting and very time-consuming once started, and could lead me away from my art career.

Our friendship progressed through the 1980s into the 1990s, and I had the pleasure of receiving at least six readings from Don. During that time I gifted him with note cards that I had designed, and he in turn gave me the books that he had written. Later I realized that he was correct in saying that once you start the mediumship work there is no turning back! So many people are hurting through the loss of loved ones. Therefore, for the last 25 years, I have dedicated my time and energy to try to bring hope, comfort and closure to them.

One cold February morning, I had the fireplace lit in the sunroom, and I wasn't at all surprised to see the spirit of Don sitting across from me. He projected in an ascot and tweed jacket and telepathically shared that spirits can create their own environments with their thought forms in Heaven. He talked about the temples of wisdom, and relayed that everyone can develop mediumship abilities if they remain dedicated to it. Don enthusiastically shared his story:

Hello my lady, this is Don. I wanted you to know how easy it was for me to cross over. After years of being a medium, as yourself, I knew intimately about the "spirit people" as I call them. I didn't plan on being a medium; I think very few people do. I think the spirit people pick who they want to talk through, and they are curious to see whether you will show the dedication and determination it takes to be a good one.

Everyone can develop the ability to converse with departed loved ones; for some it is just easier than for others. When I told you many years ago that I don't advocate that you do this work, it was because it can be time consuming and exhausting. I knew then what you'd be getting into. You are a great artist. But as you have found out, though your mediumship work helps others heal, it does not leave much time for you (as the medium) to do anything else!

But I'm so glad you're taking the time and energy to write this book about Heaven. These two worlds coincide—those of Heaven and earth. I do love the analogy you use of the mirror. The neutral back side of the mirror represents our world. We are no longer a part of the physical, third dimension, but are diaphanous spirits who can enter the earth plane at will, and sometimes use the back of the mirror as a portal. Of course you cannot be as mutable as we are, because of the dense heavy physical frequency that you reside in now.

It is quite undaunting for people to "let go" as you say, to make transition to the other side, called the soul place. You on earth are used to control. You control time and space and create what you want by working for it. We on this side are free to fly and float. When we think of a place, for example, we are suddenly there. We can astral travel through the universe and to any region of your world!

We as spirits can also *create* environments with our thought forms. These environments can be what we are used to and what we enjoyed on earth. For example, I had a special "flat" that I enjoyed in Yorkshire, England. In my flat was a small cozy room with a fireplace, a circular braided rug and English antiques. I also had a charming mantel clock, small tables to put our teacups on and comfortable overstuffed chairs with ottomans. This was a pleasant place to take afternoon tea, to sit and chat with friends and to catch up on current events. So in this world where spirits reside, I can re-create this room at will and entertain spirit people—new acquaintances and old.

I have befriended a gentleman spirit who was from India, and I invite him to tea on occasion. Quite an interesting chap, who while living on earth, was a politician of sorts. His name is Rajan. He wants to retain his Indian background for a while because he so enjoyed the Indian culture in his last incarnation. He lived on the outskirts of Nepal in India. I didn't know him when I lived on earth last time, but ironically we met at a spiritual university here. Rajan wants to study philosophy and the many ways that other cultures express themselves. I also want to continue to study because I had a penchant for reading, writing and learning. So I attended a class, and that's where we met. So you see, we can learn from scholars here at temples of wisdom, or we can learn from each other's experiences. I was always fascinated with India and now know about its culture and traditions firsthand from our meetings. I wanted to retain my British demeanor, and Rajan wanted to retain his Indian persona. When I asked him to tea he complied, so the creation of my English parlor was in order.

Ours is a world of total freedom in this soul place. There is no night or day, just eternal light and an even flow of energy. My friend, Rajan, from India has entertained me as well in a Hindu temple, which he formulated with his mind. The sunlight streams through the columns and onto the ornate marble floors, and it is decorated with red velvet divans, all with fringe at the bottom.

His petite mother, many times wearing her sarong, greets us and serves us a small meal. We graciously "go through the motions" because we cannot consume food without the physical body. But from our memories we can remember the taste of foods that we sample.

As you make friends on earth and learn from many individuals in a lifetime, we too make new friends in the spirit world and learn new things. Some spirits do not want to reincarnate immediately. They want to stay in this condition until they are ready once again to take the plunge. The physical world is wonderful, but along with the ecstasy of being in a human body, there is also the agony. You experience the aches and pains, the emotional and mental trials, the total frustrations of daily life.

We, of course, have no need for clothes, but still can project as we wish. A spirit will usually energetically retain the "form" of the physical life he or she has just left behind, not only to gain comfort without the body, but also to help retain the innate personality. I enjoy keeping my British form for now by wearing my vest, ascot and tweeds. And my new friend Rajan still looks like a nobleman from India, projecting in his favorite garb and turban while sharing his traditional customs.

Both Rajan and I will eventually choose a new life in which to incarnate. We will meet with our individual council of guides and review all past lives. This will enable us to choose a suitable set of parents, a conducive time in history and an amenable location in which to incarnate to learn our spiritual lessons. We may also select a male or female body, and even reincarnate back in time. If I physically want to learn about philosophy first hand, I can reincarnate into ancient Greece. If I want to choose a lifetime now in England to learn soul lessons as a woman, I can do so. But the process and choices have to coincide with the chosen soul lessons for that lifetime. The earth plane is quite a training ground to carry out these lessons. In the spirit world we choose to reincarnate in order to spiritually progress.

This is also the reason some people on earth have déjà vu and are drawn to different periods of history and to different countries, without consciously knowing why! For example, if you love the time frame of 1700s France, most likely you have lived there, and at that time in history.

That particular day my time was short, as I was preparing to do a phone reading, so we concluded our session.

My husband and I have an office outside of our home, where I do in-person consultations. Several months later I was sitting at my desk there and once again saw the spirit of my medium friend, Don. He continued to share information about creating environments in Heaven.

I want to talk more about how the spirit people create environments here. Anything that is developed on earth started with an idea. Now stop and look around your office. The paintings on your walls and on your easel were created by you. Where did those ideas come from? A few ideas were given to you by your spirit helpers, who have been artists or teach creative ideas here. And some painting inspirations were from your own imagination.

Your pole lamp, your heater and clock were designed from the necessity to use electricity. The earth is comprised of electrical impulses and magnetic fields. For example, these principals are used by geese to enable them to fly in a "V" formation. The knowledge to fly in formation is already in the DNA of geese, but a lot of it has to do with their ability to read the currents of electrical impulses.

You have heard the phrase, "necessity is the mother of invention," which is true. On earth you may think some people are geniuses, but actually many who thought of inventing devices (like the telephone, television or radio) were already working with the concept of electricity in the spiritual world before incarnating!

In our spirit world there is freedom to directly harness those electrical impulses. Since a spirit is electromagnetic energy, the mind can immediately create at will what it wants to create. On earth you call it the "law of attraction," as you attract what you think. It is important for people to take an accounting of their thoughts on a daily basis. Negative thinking attracts negative situations, and the same with positive thinkers who are able to produce positive results.

On your earth plane, there is the concept of time, so what you think of attracting comes to you more slowly. But here, without time constraints, what you think and visualize becomes instantly real. Not real in a physical, tangible way, but real with currents of light energy, which create light projections of whatever you wish. So a thought in the spirit realm produces an instant result!

We as human beings are one with the eternal thoughts of love, which we call the Creator. You might ask the question about exactly when your soul was created. For if you are indeed an infinite being from God, when was your beginning? What I can say is that your energetic light body has always been and will always be. Envision God as a huge flame of eternal light. When you gaze into a flame you can see sparks emanating, which would represent individual souls. The light will always glow, and you will always be a part of the light. We are never separate from God. Each spark could also represent another earthly incarnation. But no matter how many lifetimes we have had, we always return to the Source!

After you transition once again into pure love, you become a co-creator. The concept of co-creation has been challenged by religions as well as the scientific community. But truth be known (released from the low, dense energy of earth) the soul-mind is free to harness the higher frequencies of light. Thoughts are very powerful, and a person on earth can create any concept, idea, invention or career with their imagination. Remember that people are also influenced by us in the spirit world to design new things, for we are capable of sending knowledge to receptive minds.

In the spirit world without time limitations, thoughts are instantaneously creating forms. On returning here, some of the spirit people at first create gardens, mountains, mansions or other environments with their thought forms. That is their prerogative. They may do this as long as they wish. But soon spirits grow tired of creating earthly remembrances. That is when they may choose to either mentor others in this realm, or those on earth by becoming spirit guides. They may choose to teach various subjects from their own interests or life experiences, or even choose to volunteer to help spirits make transition from the physical world to this world of light.

After we are born, our spirits are limited because we are now housed in a physical body. We are not always taught on earth that there are unlimited possibilities that we can produce with our minds. But freed from the cocoon of the physical body, we are able to soar like a butterfly of light to a higher realm and spontaneously create what pleases us.

When I met my father-in-law, Oscar, there was an immediate connection. We could sit for hours talking about subjects we both loved: Asian art and artifacts, travel, music, medieval times, and even cats. He would gift me with many exotic treasures that he brought back from overseas. As a Lieutenant Colonel, Oscar had the opportunity to visit many foreign countries. My father-in-law was quite eccentric, and that's what made him so interesting. He passed away from cancer in 2001. I was elated when one day after meditating, I felt his presence, and then I saw him. He gave me information about creating environments with your mind, viewing areas and making new friends. Next is Oscar's message:

I was always fascinated with science fiction and other planets, and I was interested in the possibility of other worlds. I know now that I had long forgotten what this side was like. You know I was proud to serve our country and try to make a difference with scholarships for students and funding for education.

Well in this soul place, one thing you can do is go back and view places in history. As you go to the movies and enjoy the shows, we can view firsthand any part of history at any time, without reincarnating. I wasn't taught about reincarnation, but after having been interested in different periods in history, I thought it could be so. If you remember I was really interested in castles, medieval armies and knights.

Now I've learned that I was a knight in England (1480—1540), and in that lifetime I was also an important figure of nobility. Later, the lion and unicorn were significant symbols in the Royal Coat of Arms. The lion represented strength for England; the unicorn symbolized mysticism (there is also a Scottish version of the crest). You, Michele, were a seeress and a textile designer in that same lifetime in 1515. You created patterns and designs for fabrics and tapestries. That is why you now enjoy color, design theory and decorating. I love the medieval study that you have in your home. The stained-glass windows there always intrigued me. Incidentally, that period in history is still my favorite! The food, the costumes, the freedom to hunt in open areas, the drink called Mead, and the camaraderie around an open fire.

I must say then that because of loving that time in history, when I made transition to this world I walked into that time frame. I created that medieval environment with my mind, and there met the fair maiden that I loved, my soulmate, Minerva. She was not with me in my last lifetime as you know, but I am with her now. She has silken white skin, eyes of blue and golden curls to her waist (she is a natural blonde). I feel most at home here in this time period, so I will stay here for a while.

For me it was quite effortless to cross over. At age 94 I went for a walk, came back, sat down and died. I know you personally don't like the word "die," because you say the soul never dies—but the body does. If I could have lived the life I wanted this last time, I would have been an adventurer and traveled to every corner of the world. I would have visited every country and made many friends. I soul contracted this past life to learn humility and the simple ways of life. What is simpler than farm life? But I never enjoyed it. I felt that farm life was beneath me. So I locked myself up in my tower of books and culture. I wanted to attend operas and be a man of learning, because the responsibilities of a normal life were very boring.

There are viewing stations here, similar to your movie theaters, but our viewing stations are three-dimensional holograms. I love it here on this side. In the last 13 years of your earth time, I have first viewed, and then astrally traveled to the Orient, India, the European countries and Brazil. It's like taking a vacation. Right now I don't want to learn, I want to travel and meet other souls of like mind.

By the way, Jon (my son and your husband), was a "sentinel" on the castle wall, in our medieval lifetime together. He observed the land, much like your crows watch their area. He did not converse much for that was his job, "to watch" and protect. We knew each other, but I was of higher rank as a knight and well thought of. Jon chose me as his father from a desire to watch and learn. I could have been more loving with him, I guess, but my "position" in my own mind kept me feeling superior. I hope he understands.

My point about crossing over is that you can create what you love here, and where you want to be. My wife from my last lifetime (Jon's mother) is in a big country kitchen that she created with her mind. But as I stated, I'm free to travel and I always return to my favorite time, the 1400—1500s in Europe—from the Medieval Times to the crest of the Renaissance Period. Eventually I will leave the comfort of this era and entertain the thought of re-entering the earth plane. But I feel it won't be for a long time. As you know there is no time here, so I may not wish to return to earth for a few hundred years.

Your book is about Heaven, but there are many other worlds and star belts to explore. So for now I will try to keep my thoughts on your book's subject.

I have made new soul friends here and have actually met the spirit of General MacArthur. I have not as yet met up with General Patton, an old soul who believed in reincarnation while on earth, but I may at some point. If a soul has not already reincarnated on earth, we can set up a meeting here to have "telepathic exchange," as there is no need for talking. I have also met General Eisenhower. In my last life I had a prejudice against African Americans, I know. In my favorite medieval lifetime there were none that I met, so they were foreign to me. But I do like Colin Powell and will eventually have a telepathic exchange with him about his beliefs. This truly is what you call Heaven here—no time, no work, pure freedom to explore.

Yes, I have crossed paths with those I knew in my last life, but I want to go my own way. There will be a future lifetime chosen again for humility and simplicity, but I don't want to choose that for a while. If I seem selfish, I'm sorry. For each soul creates his own heaven, and I love mine. I know my faults and strengths, and I will hopefully learn how to soften my emotions the next time around.

For now, good day.

All my best,

Oscar

My husband's mother, Jerry, was a very loving person. She was one of eleven children from Townsend, Tennessee. Jerry was a teacher, poet and a fantastic homemaker. Her favorite color was red, and that's how she projected to me one day, wearing a red suit with a pearl necklace. My mother-in-law looked radiant and kept her message brief:

Just wanted to come by and say we are all well in Heaven and very happy. I loved nature, climbing trees, jumping over rocks and running along the creek—a tomboy I was. I have created a beautiful mountain range here in my mind, like the Smokey Mountains in Tennessee, where I grew up. We were very clannish people, so now and again our family pops down to see how you are doing on earth and to help you. I feel I lived a good life. In my life review I saw that. I like your book on prayer, Michele, and I wish I would have had that book with me in the hospital at the end of my life.

On earth I lived the simple life and want to continue that here. Although universities and traveling through other realms is interesting, I just like to sit on a bench, or sometimes in a field of daisies and watch butterflies. The world we can create here is glorious. I can also watch over my grandchildren and great grandchildren from here. I was the "peace bringer," and if I was still on earth in my physical body I would try to bring the family closer together to make peace.

I know you're writing a book on Heaven. I don't feel that I have a lot to contribute. So I will say goodbye now. I'm glad in a roundabout way that I could contribute to your visionary work, Michele, by having a wonderful boy like Jon, who is now your husband. This was all meant to be, and I'm glad for it.

Send love to everyone—have fun too.

Jerry

5

Mel's Spiritual Experiences

It was 1991, and I was beginning my work as a spiritual medium. There was a large metaphysical conference, and I was asked to participate. My reading slots were solidly booked for the week, and needless to say, I felt nervous about them. I never attended a prominent expo like this before, and I wanted to do a good job. My mission has always been about bringing healing and comfort to those who have experienced loss.

There I sat, patiently waiting in a private room for my first client. Finally a charming older gentleman walked in with a big grin, shook my hand and introduced himself. There was an immediate connection and all of my apprehension left. That was the day I met Mel, and we sustained a deep friendship for close to 16 years.

I learned that he was a professor, an author, a leading ornithologist and a well-known marine biologist. Mel traveled the country lecturing about his scientific findings on specific sea creatures and birds of the air. And he was a leading authority on ocean crustaceans, which was fascinating to learn about. Mel lived in a different state, but my husband and I were fortunate enough to visit with him and his lovely wife.

Every year he would have his annual phone consultation with me and even bought gift certificates for his wife and grown children.

During our conversations towards the end of his life, he would ask me many specific questions. What was Heaven like? What was the difference between angels and spirit guides? What was it like to cross over?

Mel passed away when he was in his mid-90s. It didn't shock me when I literally saw him sitting in the spirit chair in my sunroom, ready to communicate. His telepathic information seemed to flow effortlessly and many of the questions he had asked me before his passing were now being answered by him! The automatic writing that I received was spontaneous, and his genuine personality shone through.

Mel shared information about the levels of energy in Heaven, what soul groups are like, various temples of wisdom and learning, his life review and much more. It's an honor to share his perception of the afterlife.

Because of my close bond with Mel, I was curious about what he personally experienced after he passed away. I asked him what it was like when he left his body, and he enthusiastically shared his knowledge.

Transition

I was in my 90s and toward the end of my life I had some joint pain. I wasn't in agony but was tired physically. I had hoped at the end that I would go quickly and not be a burden on my children, and I fortunately had a smooth transition.

It was early evening and after dinner I lay down to rest. I felt like there was a tight band around my chest. With the last breath my soul literally soared above my body. It was as if my light body was saying, "Goodbye, I'm free."

As an ornithologist I always was mesmerized by birds and their ability to soar to great heights. The bird's ability to fly free fascinated me. I must say I felt lighter after passing away and recalled from the many readings I had with you, Michele, that there was quite an adventure that awaited me.

Indeed there was an exciting new world to explore. There was no looking back on earth as I sailed upward. All of a sudden, there it was—a spiraling bright light in the distance. To me it looked like a kaleidoscope, swirling with sparkling gemlike colors. I so wanted to enter this portal, was magnetized to it and then I was pulled through it! What started as gemlike colors became millions of iridescent sparkles, still swirling around me.

Then everything became bright, white light that I instantaneously realized my human eyes could never gaze upon. It was like looking into the heart of the sun but much more radiant.

My soul kept moving forward and then I saw them—my beloved parents, grandparents and great grandparents! My dearest ancestors appeared. I *knew* them by their form, which of course was not a physical one, but a form of "soul recognition." Instead of embracing, we *melded* our energy together. I could at once meld with them all to feel their spirits, and it was truly sublime.

I started to sense new entities, and soon others appeared, all from my specific soul group in Heaven. It was comforting to know they recognized me and I them. I instantly *knew* what lifetimes we had shared and why they chose to be my guides and mentors. Each individual soul that I encountered had an aura of a different hue. There were souls who had violet light surrounding them, while some emanated pulsating royal blue light or soft pink light, and still others glistened in bright gold. Then I understood at once that each one had a "soul color" that their energy aligned with.

The beings with amethyst purple light were very evolved souls that I had the pleasure of spending time with in past lives. The light bodies with royal blue auric fields were watching over me and indeed had shown protection to me during many incarnations. Then there were the souls with soft, rose pink light. I recognized that they were feminine, nurturing spirits who gave me pure unconditional love. The most astounding souls were the ones with bright golden light surrounding them, and I knew them to be my *higher* guides. They were of the ascended master energy, advocates of the "Christ Consciousness."

I remained in the presence of these evolved beings for a transcendent amount of time, basking in the recognition and peace I felt. There was no urgency to move on, for I could meld with their sublime energy for as long as I wished. At that moment there was no need to visualize meadows, mountains or oceans, as others may have done. These beings of light did not beckon me to come with them, but I intuitively *knew* it was time to objectively view the life that I had just left behind.

It was interesting to remember that I had experienced this process before. My book of life was shown after my other past lives, so I was happily prepared to follow them. My life review was very succinct and defined. I was standing in the center of a horseshoe shaped glass table. Gathered around the table were a number of new spirit beings that I intuitively saw as my "council." This group of beings was a form of collective consciousness that had never lived on the earth plane. The group happened to be highly evolved and was my personal entourage! Some people would call them angels, because they are definitely not human souls. The frequency of this collective consciousness is much higher, and they cannot be perceived on earth. Behind them was a huge screen, and what appeared on it was my past life, from beginning to end. I understood all that had been and will be. I melded my energy with the Godhead and once again became one with all that is.

The lessons for my last lifetime were to be a patient teacher, a devoted researcher and an informative writer. Balance in all areas of my life was necessary, and I was to share the knowledge I had acquired. I tried to consciously balance my mind with prayer and meditation. I had agreed to treat my body as a temple with good nutrition and moderation. In my previous life I had learned self-discipline and was aware of not emotionally hurting anyone while on earth. The spiritual council asked me if I was satisfied with the life I had lived and if I thought my soul purpose was fulfilled. I answered yes! I was only asked that one question, yet somehow I knew in my spirit that other souls may have been asked a myriad of questions in their life review, but mine was simple.

I fortunately was aware of entering my past lifetime with a dose of humility, which kept me balanced when I was honored with the books I had written and the extensive marine biology research I had done. I was then eager to explore this new world which we call *home*.

A few days later, after my prayer and meditation session, I felt Mel wanted to continue. I opened my eyes, and his spirit once again was sitting across from me.

I was always curious about the great beyond and you helped me prepare for it, with our numerous sessions. I thought I knew what to expect, but this place where souls reside is even more magnificent! While living on earth I was interested in ornithology (the study of birds) and marine biology. From the many books I authored I assumed the wildlife and marine life energy here would be similar, and yet I didn't know. Well in this frequency, through sheer telepathy, you can "commune" with many different species—including mollusks. When I refer to commune, I mean you can actually become one with the energy of the bird or octopus. You are not them of course, but you can feel their energy and understand them from a deep cellular level.

There is an informative group of scientists here, and I like to meet with them. One soul was an astronomer, one a physicist, another a biologist and others like me who studied sea mammals and birds. I have learned much about this dimension and how it coincides with the earth plane. What people can't see or feel they many times dismiss. Thank heavens we have true visionaries, like you, who can tap into this soul place.

Michele, you wisely use the analogy of a ceiling fan to explain the difference between worlds. When the ceiling fan is turned off the blades become dense still matter, and you can count them. This represents the slower, denser frequency of the earth plane. But, when turned on high speed, the frequency of the fan changes and you cannot perceive the blades, yet they are still there. This higher, faster frequency represents Heaven.

Now think of the earth as a dense heavy ball, much like the energy of the fan while turned off. There is a faster frequency that surrounds the earth. This dimension of light is vast and infinite with no time or space. We call it the soul place. Here we do not eat, drink or sleep. There is no need for physical aspects without the physical body. With this freedom a soul has a vast array of things to do and learn, without time constraints.

There are spiritual temples of wisdom and learning, which are created from a mass soul consciousness. Inventors and artists can actually form soul groups in which to interact. Musicians and writers use the same concept. Architects instill innovative ideas to other souls about structural designs to influence earthly minds. Souls can learn these things from either groups of other experienced souls or by attending schools of learning. As you say, "There are as many things to do in this dimension spiritually as there are things to do on earth in physical form."

Souls cannot consume food or drink, but even the memories of this enjoyment can bring back a form of taste or smell, which is quite pleasant. As was stated, we can meld our energy with another soul for sublime ecstasy if we so choose. This process of merging would be similar to lovemaking in your world, but better, because we can become totally one.

There is no day or night, just eternal love and light. We can take as long as we want to study a subject here, because we have the luxury of no time constraints. There are vast libraries that hold records and information on all subjects. We can immediately imbibe the information and can retain it. An exceptionally brilliant earthborn soul may have studied many subjects before incarnating. We are aware that certain souls choose to become adept at just one subject like art or music. Creativity and imagination are revered here and are easy to accomplish with just thought forms.

We do not actually "speak" to each other; we telepathically send information to each other's minds. The mind is very different from the physical brain. The mind is soul-based; the brain is a part of the physical constitution, and therefore we no longer have need for a brain. We use thought transference, there is no need for words so there is not a language barrier. We have a "universal language" that we know and use.

If on earth there were deformities of the physical body, they are not shown here. What is shown here is the brilliant "light body" of the soul. No illness or negativity can reside in this realm. There are spirit counselors and psychologists who have learned how to deal with dysfunctional issues while living on earth. If a soul perceives personal flaws or idiosyncrasies in their life review, they can request to be mentored by spirit counselors. They will then understand why they acted or reacted in a certain way. The spiritual mind has no mental disorders, no bipolar, schizophrenia or manic depressive behavior. I must add, however, that this soul place is not a fairyland.

Levels of Heaven

Not all spirits arrive here at the same level. In what you call Heaven, there are different strata of energy. These higher frequencies are not linear, but they are overlapping.

Now think of Heaven as similar to the overlapping layers of an onion. The core is a denser dimension or frequency with not much light. It is comprised of a gray, foggy matter. Those people's spirits, who committed horrible crimes, go there first. Also, discarnate entities or earthbound spirits can occupy this area. These are disembodied beings that have not ascended to the light. As you move through frequencies to the outer skin of the onion, you will find the bright and pure light of the Creator. When the life-force leaves the body at death it travels and is transformed to its original state, which is energy. Some souls are not aware that their physical body is gone since they can still feel, hear and see in a spiritual sense. Sometimes spirits, because they don't *believe*, have to be convinced that there is a beautiful afterlife. They have to *remember.*

When a newborn takes the first breath, the light body, which is eternal, will enter the infant. The newborn is starting a new life with new experiences and new soul lessons to learn. Therefore, knowledge of this soul place is forgotten. When an infant sleeps a lot, that soul is trying to adjust to the denser energy of the earth plane. As you say at your seminars, the formative years—one to five—are when children see and hear spirits from our world and can communicate with them. The soul in a child's body can come and go, because it has not been contained in its physical shell for very long.

The purpose of each new life that a soul chooses is to gain earthly information and a new perspective on their soul journey. Souls may be easily derailed from their pre-chosen purpose or mission. Temptation to indulge in a decadent, materialistic or lustful life is always enticing while in the physical body. Through being separate from the source of love, fear, phobias and confusion may set in. And sometimes the pre-chosen physical bodies are imperfect (with physical disabilities) because their DNA is linked to a certain line of genealogy. This is where physical or mental illness may occur. The soul uses the body to gain mobility and learn lessons. All souls were created in love, equality and perfection. When free choice was given to humankind as a gift is when physical imperfection occurred.

Returning to the concept of Heaven being like layers of an onion, there is a denser, core frequency for criminal minds that need rehabilitation. Many tend to sleep there as they do not remember the warmth of love or the beauty of the light. Eventually (and it may take many years of earth time), they do awaken and understand where they are. They cannot transmute their energy into oneness again until after their life review, which gives them truth and understanding.

Next, there is a slightly higher energy frequency for some of those who take their life. They need to accept, understand and take responsibility for their actions. Even though this action is a choice, the soul may not have fulfilled its original contract or agreement for its time on earth.

With the help of our guides we choose situations on earth for growth. We choose parents and locations in which to be born to further our learning. The earth is a "training ground." It seems as if some people have charmed lives while others have intense problems and tragedies. This is hard to fathom, but many times a soul will choose a dire earth plane situation to progress spiritually.

There is *oneness* and *pure love* in the light with the Creator. We do not have this consistent bliss on earth, although many ascended ones have come to earth to teach the principles of love. One was the Christ who epitomized light, love, healing, forgiveness, renewal and acceptance of one another. Buddha preached oneness in peace with the Source—which is the Creator. Many saints and other ascended masters have traversed the earth plane as examples of compassion and love. We are to learn from these principles and try to use them in our daily lives. Enlightenment, truth and awakening of the soul (while inhabiting a human body) is of utmost importance.

The next month I felt Mel's presence in my sunroom for a few days, but didn't have the chance to communicate with him. When I finally did, he was the gentleman he always was, and so we started once again:

Soul Choices for a New Earth Lifetime

I'd like to talk about the "total freedom" we feel here. We can soul progress at our leisure, and don't have to learn or study immediately. People on earth tend to put other people into classes or groups of society. Some feel that if a person is uneducated or poor, that they are *less* of a person. This is true especially in America—the land of opportunity. I have observed from here that many strive for power, wealth, position and fame. But I must say, although it's difficult to conceive, we are all equal. A number of souls choose to be born into poverty on earth, so they can understand the dynamics of being poor. They want to be aware of how people are treated by society in that condition. There may be those living in poverty who feel they are treated better by receiving grants, food stamps and the like. Conversely, others feel like victims and that life has dealt them a bad deal. It's all a matter of individual perception.

When a soul decides to incarnate again, it chooses everything for spiritual progression, making contracts before birth. With the help of our guides and past life knowledge, we choose our parents, our sex, our environment and certain situations in which to incarnate. The parents we choose do not necessarily have to be nurturing. If a soul chooses to learn self-determination and self-assertion, then coddling is not the answer. If, on the other hand, a soul needs to see and learn about devotion and compassion, they will choose parents who are nurturing and loving.

The soul journey that I speak of has nothing to do with perfection (though it may seem so). The true essence of the journey is love, *and* it is *most important* to include loving self. The spark of the Divine Creator is in each human being. So there needs to be a balance between loving others and loving self. The Christian religion says "do unto others as you would have them do unto you." But in a sense, loving yourself is also synonymous with loving others. To love others only is to deny self and the divine spark within, which is God. The soul's ultimate experience then, is a balance of honoring and loving God, loving self and loving others. When this totality of love can be achieved, the soul is fulfilled and at peace. Ultimately, the soul which finally feels this total peace (after many lifetimes), does not wish or need to incarnate again. At this point in the journey the soul may chose to teach in the spirit realm.

Teachers on earth are sometimes underrated, but not here! Teachers are valued as examples of pure love. And when I first spoke of freedom, I meant a spirit is unencumbered by pain, any form of limitation or the physical body. We are pure energy and as energy we can transmute, be different places at once, learning various subjects at once.

The ability of the soul to splinter off and transmute its energy to different places is a thought provoking idea. So if a soul chooses to learn more about art and painting, which is the true expression of a human being, then that soul can study different painting styles all at once. This may be difficult for you on earth to fathom, since the longer you live on earth, the more you forget.

Rescue Teams

There are also souls here called "rescue teams." Souls band together to create a strong energy force to magnetize other souls to the light when they cross over together en masse. For example, the World Trade Center tragedy on September 11, 2001 is such a case. Although groups of souls exited at once, most were filled with fear. A light body needs to be extricated from fear before he or she can once again enter our world of light. The thousands of light bodies in this realm who agreed to be part of the rescue teams formed a dense circle of energy around Ground Zero. They urged these frightened souls, who passed from tragedy, to come with them. Most did, but a couple may still linger there. They may still be confused, afraid or maybe did not believe in an afterlife. Our belief systems initially remain with us immediately after we pass on; so tragic circumstances may cause a fearful soul to cling to earth. Eventually, through prayer and the heavenly rescue teams, all will enter the light.

The rescue teams who volunteer consist mainly of spirit beings who have passed in tragic situations themselves. The three days of the Civil War in Gettysburg, Pennsylvania during July 1863 is another example of a large group of souls leaving earth en masse in a horrifying and shocking way. Some wounded soldiers lingered in pain and eventually died. The lucky ones joined us quickly on this side, assisted by spiritual rescue teams.

Whether it's a war situation, a massive tidal wave, earthquake, tsunami or other natural disasters, spiritual rescue teams from here come down to help souls make transition. As we soul contract a chronological timeline to live on earth, those people whose time is not up will survive these occurrences. When a tragic condition happens on earth, be encouraged to pray for those departed souls to once again find the light of God.

Ascended Masters and Temples of Learning

I want to take a brief moment to talk about the ascended masters and the new colleagues I've met. As you meet new people on earth and bond with them, you can also meet new spirit friends in this world. As we can attract people of "like mind" on earth, we do the same with other light bodies here!

The physical brain dies, but the life force of the soul mind never can be destroyed. Contained in one's soul mind are memories, the ability to learn and study and the ability to lead groups of other souls through this accumulated wisdom.

There are "Temples of Wisdom and Learning," and these majestic structures have been created as a hologram by a collective "group consciousness." These structures house advanced light beings called ascended masters. If a soul, while inhabiting a physical body, has shown works of benevolence, been aware of humility and stayed in the realm of unconditional love through many incarnations, that soul is vibrating at a higher frequency which moves that soul into the "ascended master" status. The ascended masters are capable of teaching groups of souls who want to learn about any subject. For example temples of creativity are here for us to learn about painting techniques, musical composition, design concepts, architecture and literature.

We are never forced to do or think in a restricted way in this realm. There is no religious, political or racial prejudice. We enter into the collective consciousness of the Godhead. So please remember, while on earth, every loving, uplifting thought helps to raise the energy of the earth plane. Every negative, angry thought pulls down the energy of the earth. Guard your thoughts and be aware of them!

Advanced artists, philosophers and inventors from times past—Leonardo da Vinci, Plato and Einstein—do not wish to reincarnate to earth again, choosing to stay here to teach the principles they have learned. Thus these "older souls," who have had more earthly incarnations, no longer need or want to re-enter the training ground that you call earth.

I personally am still interested in literature, writing, teaching, ornithology and marine biology. Those who were pioneers in these fields who passed on before me, are now teaching me!

I may eventually choose to come down again to earth with new knowledge to help humanity. For now, I'm very content because the desire for food, drink and lovemaking release their grip on us in this realm. There are no distractions, just peace and total "free choice" to learn and progress.

Soul groups

Soul groups indeed exist! Michele, I am part of your soul group. We had a lifetime together in Egypt and one in the ancient Aztec culture. We were always bonded, and when I first met you I felt an instant connection at the metaphysical expo back in 1991. I was your first reading at the event—remember? Well, I lived a good life, into my 90s, and you helped me prepare for what was to come when I had my annual consultation. It's quite a pleasure to work with you now, and I am happy to oblige.

A soul group is a gathering of souls with a common thread, bond or interest. This group evolves over time in your earth parameter. With every lifetime we cross paths with many other people. Some people, we instantly feel a connection to, while others we tend to forget. In your present incarnation for example, your parents, grandparents, half-sister, maternal uncle, a few clients (like me) and a couple friends are from your soul group. As we make soul agreements to incarnate together, we are also learning lessons from each other and teaching each other.

A person who doesn't get along with their siblings may think, "Why would I choose them?" Even though their actions may be hurtful, you are learning valuable soul lessons, and they are teaching you insightful new understandings. Of course not everyone you cross paths with in a lifetime is from your soul group. But the ones you get along with, or the ones who "push your buttons" for a consistent amount of time, usually are.

I'd like to use your teaching career as an example of a soul contract. Since you taught art in public schools, can you remember your various principals? Did you bond with some or have problems with others? I can tell you that your first female principal is from our soul group. Although she seemed mean-spirited and demanding, she taught you the art of survival and independence, which was your soul contract with her. She taught you how to yield, get along with others and compromise. The other principals taught you nothing. Therefore, during a lifetime, there may be thousands of people who you will meet in passing and even some who you may stay with for an extended amount of time. And while some of them are from your soul group, most are not.

It may be difficult for you on earth to fathom infinity. Father/Mother God, the Supreme Being is infinite, the universe is infinite and the energy of your soul is infinite. Your life force has always been and always will be. Your spirit essence can never be destroyed.

Many souls from your group do not necessarily incarnate with you each lifetime. You may have taught them lessons or learned from them during a past lifetime. Others did not choose to be on earth ever again, but stay in this realm and help other souls or themselves to advance.

Soul groups vary in size, and individual souls can rotate their incarnations with you. If you think of the billions of people now living on earth, you can understand that there is little chance that you would have known all of them.

Let's talk about boyfriends, girlfriends, husbands, wives and casual lovers. Not everyone who you have had an intimate relationship with is necessarily from your soul group. A "one night stand" for example could just be another example of two ships passing in the night, while a 50 year marriage would indicate that your spouse is a member of your group. Soul group members are usually in your present life for quite a few years, because you are learning from them and/or teaching them. And then some incarnate just to help you progress professionally.

The average soul group (opposed to what you might think) can be from about 500 to 10,000 or more souls! If you look objectively at the populace of the world and how many incarnations you can have with these various souls, you will understand it's not just a handful, but a substantial group! As was stated, within this group you make agreements and choose future parents, children, spouses, friends, coworkers, clients, neighbors and others for spiritual progression.

Michele, think of the thousands of clients who you have personally awakened or helped. Now stop and think who you specifically remember and count them. I'm only referring to your clients, whether living or deceased. Who stands out? I think you just counted 15 to 20 that you remember. Why? Because they are from your soul group. The many other clients who you've counseled came for you to "awaken" them to the truth that we don't die, that love is eternal.

A soul group can expand with new members, but it can never be minimized or diminished. With each new spiritual encounter, whether it's in Heaven or on earth, there's a karmic cord that brings your members together.

If you're in New York City and walk by hundreds of people, most likely they are not connected to you. But if you have a lifetime friend in New York City who you have exchanged ideas and life itself with, then it is likely that your friend is a member of your soul group. When a human thinks of the term "group," he or she tends to categorize people. They may think of a specific racial group, a tribe of Native American Indians, or even people with the same profession like doctors or janitors. Taken another direction, a person may group together all of the feline species, whether they be big cats or domestic pets. We tend to put people and animals into specific groups that we see as similar. However, each individual from a group whether human or animal, has a distinct personality. But soul groups are different. Even though each soul within the group retains a personality, they are androgynous light bodies who are exclusively and continually magnetized to each other and learn from each other, while physically on earth and spiritually in Heaven.

It's been wonderful to share this information with you, Michele. I will now say farewell.

Blessings to you, my dear friend and thank you,

Mel

6

Teaching Entertainment

One sunny autumn morning I was in my spiritual conversation room and said a simple protective prayer. When I looked up, sitting in the spirit chair was a gorgeous light body of a woman. I recognized her immediately as a very famous singer while she was on earth. This beauty wore a low-cut, long red, sequined gown with gold sandals. Her complexion was radiantly glowing, and then she spoke:

Entertainment

Music and Singing

Miel—I'll call you that—it means "honey" or "sweet" in French, and you are sweet. First, the beauty in this dimension is unreal. I am one with all that is. This is a place of radiant color, some of the colors I never saw before when I was on earth. Orbs are constantly moving and very bright with tremendous light patterns in different rays. You can actually become the ray of light and color. Nothing is separate; all is one with love—with God. I thought Heaven would be much different. I think we all forget what it's like here; we forget where we have come from. You can't be in two worlds at *once*! This place is home, our *real* home. The earth is just a stage to learn lessons and like you say, Miel, it's a place to learn to give love, love yourself and be aware of compassion. I see that your "heart light" is kind. It's cool to see people's heart light from here. There are people who have a small "pilot light" flickering—a little flame in their hearts. Others have a fire cooking, and, like you, some have a blaze of sparkle, a lighthouse beacon of piercing light that changes things and people.

I like the concept of your book on Heaven. From what I've seen, I guess you'd call me a young soul. I was able to love my family but had a hard time loving others. I enjoyed my fans, but now I see I was self-centered. I indulged myself in everything I wanted and I wanted everything. I grew up Christian, so had a strong belief in Jesus. So of course when I went towards the light I saw Him. At first I hovered around my body in disbelief. I actually tried to force my soul back into my body, but that was impossible. My body that I viewed below was pale and lifeless; my eyes were still open, and I looked old. I thought to myself, "Am I dead?" It was strange because above me and somewhat to the right was a round sunbow looking orb. I loved the colors and was curious. I felt very free, like a bird set free for the first time from its cage. I noticed that I could fly it seemed higher and higher. I was still curious about the "shell" of the body I left behind, but this glow beckoned me; the light called my first name, and it felt familiar. Then I somehow knew if I could fly there, I could also come back to the area below. The "area below" as I now call it was earth. On earth my time was rather short, but I had a dream life. Not with relationships necessarily, but with success. It seemed everything I touched turned to gold.

In Heaven music and singing are so vital and important for souls to hear and imbibe. There are sound frequencies here that you don't have on earth. When someone says a person "sings like a bird," it pales in comparison to what we hear in Heaven. As there are colors here that can't be perceived on earth, the vibration of sound currents is awesome as well. A soul can actually stand in a frequency of sound waves for enlightenment or for meditation. People said I had a "God given talent" and voice; but in a way, that came from many years (in your earth time) of study here in Heaven.

My heart was pure when I was born, but the temptations of the world lured me. I did not honor myself;

I took for granted my abilities. When things come easy, you don't question. Other people may say, "Oh my God, you are so lucky to have that gift." But being in your own skin, if it comes too easy like that, you take it for granted. And years of self abuse ruined my voice while on earth. It wasn't a life wasted 'cause people still listen to my music, but I let a lot of people down.

So what am I doing now? Well I check in on my family. There are a couple ways we can still connect with those we love while up here in Heaven. We can view our loved ones as a hologram at viewing stations or we can travel back down to earth for a short time. It is hard to hold the higher frequency of your soul down on earth, once you cross over. So we can meet those we love halfway in dreams. Their souls come up here, and we come down and meet them halfway. The frequency here is too high for a soul still in a physical body to handle. And our souls, from here, can only hold our energy down towards earth for a few minutes at a time. That's why dreams of us here are short and sweet. Certain souls have not made it to Heaven, you know the ones still "earthbound," the "discarnates" as you call them. They hang around the places they knew on earth, so you don't dream of them as much.

Teachers are revered here, and many souls teach, but I'm not spiritually evolved enough to teach. I'm not an old soul. With that I mean I've only had several earthly lifetimes. I've learned about the importance of music and sharing it from those past lifetimes. First, concepts are created with your thoughts here, then I learned how to bring my singing tones down to the earth. Singing was like breathing for me; it was that easy. "Runs" were like breathing too (the ability to raise and lower your voice) because I practiced in Heaven, and it was effortless to bring that ability through.

When a human soul can physically bring down ideas for art, architecture, design, creative writing or music in any form, the angels sing. Although science is wonderful, nothing soothes the human soul like the arts. I wish I could tell people on earth that it's not about the clothes you wear, the money you have, or the fame or even education. What it's truly about is sharing what you've learned from this side, and being kind to people. Kindness is underrated on earth, but here we view kindness as the same as love. I see now that I could have been kinder.

Now in Heaven I'm again studying the frequencies of music. Singing will always be a part of my soul. As artists want to create and paint, singers must sing. On this side there are heavenly choirs, not always of angels, but of human souls! We work with "vibrations" because we no longer have a physical body or voice. Through telepathy and joining together, we create different musical vibrations. All I can compare it to is different people on earth humming together. With these musical frequencies, we also can create harmonizing colors with our soul minds. I think it's important that artists who paint listen to music while they are creating.

The spectrum of colors here (which are more varied and advanced than earth colors), vibrate with sound frequencies too. When a group of us with "like minds" harmonize musical vibrations, the sound is supremely beautiful. We are not taught "how to sing" because again we no longer have the physical body. But we are taught by "musical masters" how to create different tones with our minds. When gifted singers are born, they bring to earth those higher vibrations. By doing so, the tones are more pleasing when a song is sung.

Artists may try to capture the "colors" of our heavenly world, but they are so vivid and intense that no artist, as far as I know, has really captured that saturated intensity. So we don't go to music school; we practice with other souls to make a "musical consciousness," which you on earth would call a choir.

Sometimes when a person is about to cross over they hear singing. Well, some of us choose to let people hear us before they pass away. I guess you'd call us "musical volunteers."

I also want to add that prayer is powerful, so keep praying. People on earth should also pray for our souls here. It brings us peace. There is a "force of love"—it is a force to be reckoned with. Love conquers, love heals, love creates, love never dies. I'm learning here about the force of love and how to move that powerful force to earth!

I'm now relaxing after a long day of lecturing and doing consults at a resort in the Poconos when I hear a bold spirit voice say, Sarah! I really don't hear a voice, I must be imagining things, I think to myself. Then the phone rings; it's the concierge desk. I hear, "Hi, I'm Sarah and here is your schedule for tomorrow." So with that little confirmation I was prepared to write. This time I did not "see" a spirit, only heard a voice.

Theater and Creativity

Michele, this is Sarah. I was a theatrical person with my career culminating in the early 1900s. When I say theatrical, I mean flamboyant—ahead of my time and very innovative. Most artists are all of these things that I just mentioned. In childhood you may be told what not to do, but as time progresses you need to be yourself. I feel you need to honor your true mission and honor your gifts. In my era women were not that flamboyant or "out there;" and I did have some masculine tendencies as well. In my time (late 1800s to early 1900s) these tendencies were known as independence, self-assurance and freedom from control.

As a girl, I loved to perform for family and friends. We all make mistakes, but even as a girl, the thought of male attention was intoxicating! But be that as it may, I followed my heart and I chose to shine, shine, shine. I am addressing the concept of creative people on earth—whether they be actors, artists, musicians. Many artistic high-minded people have been put down, criticized for their work and told they were crazy. Now I'm not alluding to mediums, as yourself; I'm acknowledging artistic temperaments in general. Well-known authors also have had their share of adversity. I'm here and communicating to say I so enjoyed the theater and the recognition I received. There is nothing like the "sound of applause" after a job well done! One might say this euphoric feeling is vanity, but I will say that it's important to shine in whatever creative capacity you find yourself.

In this next world of Heaven, I teach theatrical ways of approaching life. Not life lived on earth as rote or life as a fabric woven of religion, hypocrisy or prejudice, but life as a way of "freedom of expression"—as individuality. Yes, some may even question your work (as a medium and an artist)—those of narrow indoctrinated minds. So be it!

Theater and entertainment are so important, both in Heaven and on earth. Here we have troubadours trained to entertain, who will be future actors and comedians in their next incarnation on earth. They train to make us happy, to take the cares of the world off our shoulders and to create laughter—and not just for diversion. As there are addicted gamblers, alcoholics and so called philanderers on earth, I must say that entertainers are a "sweet narcotic." Entertainers such as dancers, musicians or comedians may be addictive to the populace, but not as addictive as drugs or alcohol! A comedian brings laughter and relief, and a dancer or performer on the Broadway stage also brings escape. This escape—for a moment or an hour—is so important for people. Through that laughter, there is hope and an alleviation of the days worries.

A star can seem bigger than life itself, but all people on earth have the same insecurities, setbacks and travesties. So here in this place which you on earth call Heaven, there is entertainment. Who does not want to be amused? There are so-called schools to learn the craft of entertainment in any form (music, dancing, singing, comedy), and one can study with the "greats" of entertainment here.

Actors are trained in this realm to play a part or amuse us. True entertainers possess gifts to enthrall. These gifts have been honed from older souls who have had many past lives involving their craft. So on earth entertainment is an escape for people to relish and imbibe.

We have classes here, and I myself am a teacher of the craft of instructing actors. I love that there are no time constraints here. And since there is no time here, a laugh will always be a laugh; a cry will always be a cry; a moment of entertainment will always grip a captive audience. And for one giving the public these things, it is euphoric—beyond measure.

As far as I'm concerned I know there are scientists, physicians, chemists and the like. All of these professions are valuable. But to escape the mundane, to transcend the average, to be placed among a higher cause or just merely to entertain—to me that is of the highest order.

Sincerely,
Sarah

The next spirit (who was a Jewish comedian on earth) really caught me off guard, not just with his personal story, but with his big personality. He was also very direct on his views of life, his religion and the afterlife:

Comedy

I'm introducing myself as a Jewish comedian, popular from the 1950s and onward. As a Jew, I did not believe in an afterlife, and as our people were persecuted by Hitler, there was an underlying aftermath of anger and so-called revenge. At times in history we were meant to feel inferior, but for God's sake remember, even Jesus was a Jew! I come to you to tell you my story—not of persecution, but of love.

There was a small town near Brooklyn, outside of Manhattan, that was known as the "Jewish Community." There we talked about food, politics and family. In every city and town there is a section where the Jews congregate. In these Jewish communities, we felt safe and knew everyone else. We believed that Jesus was a great prophet but not a savior. At least my family believed this. We were trying to forgive the Germans; although we knew Hitler was a lunatic, we still (as a people) couldn't believe the devastation that occurred during the war. My paternal great aunt and uncle endured the camps; my uncle died in the gas chamber. My great aunt was able to somehow survive the Holocaust and live to tell about it. She was 93 when she passed away and an icon for our family. The horrors she saw were unspeakable, not only of starvation, but of verbal and mental cruelty. Nightmares plagued her for many years. I want to say our people (maybe unconsciously) have felt persecuted and denied the rights of passage for many years.

As far as I am concerned, the "Aryan Race" does not exist! A blonde, blue-eyed person is not superior to a brown eyed, dark-haired person. This is hypocrisy—this is insanity. The Jewish population, as I see it from this side, has been trying to prove themselves for a long time. To prove that we are worthy, intelligent and deserving. Our belief system does not match Christianity. Some of us believe, in essence, when you're dead, you're dead. Now some in our Jewish faith may disagree with me, but growing up near Brooklyn, that's how it was. Many Jews are comedians, and I think we have used this trade in entertainment as a means to escape the negativity and horror that has infiltrated our populace.

But you want to hear about Heaven—the next world. Some of us may not believe in the hereafter, but we believe in family, tradition and in our heritage. Fanny Brice, the great performer and comedian, was a part of my era—a woman who knew herself, an independent being who was not afraid of life and was not shrinking in the shadows. I modeled myself after her in my career. "Keep them laughing and keep them guessing," was my motto.

Well, now I know there is a hereafter and some Jews on earth may argue this point. Heaven is what you believe it to be. You don't have to prove yourself here, and you don't have to be angry. This is a place of camaraderie, family ties and learning. My father was a good attorney, and my two brothers went to school for higher education. I may have been the so-called "black sheep," but I made more money than all of them put together. As I said (and in my opinion), we've been trying to make up for persecution ever since the war. I feel that it is an unconscious drive with many Jews, but it's there.

Laughter is the best medicine, and you may not think that you can learn how to be comedic here, but you can. I know this well because I have chosen to teach souls about comedy! Comedy in its pure essence is a childlike phenomenon. Children are innately funny; they don't censor. We can laugh at others, but the greatest laughs are about ourselves. Over here, I am objective. I call a spade a spade. There is an area created by me that is like a canteen. Canteens were popular during the war; they were places that anyone from Bob Hope to Bing Crosby would perform and make them laugh. And yes, although Crosby was a crooner, he and Bob Hope together stole the show.

So I'll admit I was an atheist on earth. How could a God put so many precious Jews—our people—to death for no reason? But now I understand the real hell *is* earth—plain and simple. Earth is a training ground for your soul to learn your higher purpose. Here I can still make'em laugh and teach souls who want to learn the "art of comedy" to let themselves go and to "live comedy" the way they lived life. For every day on earth there is something to laugh about. People on earth need to know, see and feel the positive aspects of laughter. I have observed that so many on earth are stuck in self-pity and anger, and need to laugh more.

Along with me, there are many "old school" comedians here who had a natural gift of improv. They also teach, if souls want to learn comedy. Yes, impromptu comedy is a gift and an ability that some have. It is not just a so-called good sense of humor.

Comedy is important in Heaven. Laughter is joyous and paramount. You might think that an angel might "gets his wings" when a bell rings, like in the movie *It's a Wonderful Life*. But this I know: a laugh brings happiness and even more joy to souls in this world which you call Heaven. And so comedy is one of the most important arts to teach and to learn. And I must say, in my opinion, that the Jews have it cornered!

As I was working on this book, not all spirit interactions happened in the designated sunroom. When I was alone and my mind was in neutral, the kitchen also became a popular place for communication. I was in my kitchen making a cup of tea and heard singing. It was a popular song from the 1960s, and I hummed along. Then I distinctly heard and recognized the female singing voice. I felt her energy and knowing that specific information was going to come through, I once again was prepared to do some spontaneous writing. While I headed to the sunroom to write, she was still singing that snappy and happy song. I sat down, took a deep breath, and this is the message I received:

Music, Singing and Dance

Hi, I would like to talk about the aspect of singing on this side. We cannot physically sing of course, but our spirits can study tonal qualities and actually step into tonal frequencies to feel their vibrations. The great singers, who lived on earth and shared their singing voice with others, can teach us here about the frequencies of tone. We can become spiritual "tuning forks" and our progression has to do with vibrations. A spirit can imbibe tone, and if it is pleasing, that spirit can vibrate with its frequency and call it their own. It becomes their "soul tone."

Both my husband and I were singers, and we enjoyed performing together. Even though he seemed pleasant while we worked together, behind the scenes he was demanding and liked the ladies—which just happened to be ALL other ladies. I knew about his affairs, but looked the other way because of our careers together. I loved singing as a child, but it was hard to break into show business—a good agent always helps. My performing brought me great joy and happiness.

Not all singers who lived on earth want to teach about music when they come over to this world. Some spirits want to rest or learn about other areas of interest. Believe it or not, dance is popular here too. Without the encumbrance of the physical body, we're totally free to twirl, jump, fly and be free. Ballerinas who had prominent careers on earth with dance, can teach other spirits the basics. Spirit dancers can also merge their energy fields with others to form a collective consciousness of dance, which is pleasing for them and also for us to watch.

Musical compositions are created with telepathic thought forms while entering tonal frequencies. Composers then try to influence receptive minds on earth with their musical ideas. You know the term "muse," but some great pianists like Chopin and Beethoven were truly inspired by ascended master musicians from this side. Music, singing, dance and creating musical compositions are very much revered here.

I'd also like to discuss rhythm. The aspect of rhythm is so important for balancing our souls. Think of the ocean —the tides come to shore and recede—never too soon or too late. The oceans' flow is in perfect rhythm. So musical timing is crucial for composers. I enjoyed jazz and bossa nova because there was an underlying snap or consistency to the compositions. Even today's rap (which I don't care for) has its own unique rhythm.

I wanted to contribute to your book because I feel more needs to be mentioned about singing, dancing and the musical arts. Chambers can be created here by mental thought forms that vibrate with all of the musical notes, along with new frequencies that are not heard or perceived on earth. This is a magical world, filled with so many wonderful things to do and learn.

You've heard the phrase she "sings like a bird." Well here we can observe the avian (bird) consciousness. Birds are masters of tonal frequencies and some spirits try and copy them. By doing this, many become opera singers in future lifetimes. Birds truly are "symbols of the soul." They are happy joy bringers that have the ability (like our souls) to fly free!

Thanks for listening and writing down what I dearly wanted to share. I'm glad you heard my voice singing to you. An angelic voice can lift someone's spirit on earth, and harmonious singing will always soothe the savage beast within.

My husband Jon and I have visited many Caribbean islands over the years but have returned to Jamaica seven times. We love the little resort on beautiful Negril Beach, where we always stay. Although we like reggae music, I never thought about the "King of Reggae" communicating with me, probably because during past trips I wasn't writing a book on Heaven. However, one morning after breakfast my husband walked down to the beach, leaving me sitting alone in the open-air gazebo. I looked up and sitting across from me at the table was the spirit of a Jamaican reggae master! I knew he wanted to communicate, so I quickly asked one of the servers for a pen and reached for some paper napkins. To my astonishment, this is what I received:

Music and Entertainment

Hey Mon, I want to talk to you about the "joy of music." Music was in my soul from the time I was little. There was rhythm along the beach and in the mountains. I was always dancing with my brother and clapping. I hurt a lot in my soul, for my people of Jamaica. It's not that I wanted to shine, but I was a part of them—the culture and the traditions. Many here have a "chip on their shoulder" as you in the Americas would say. But we have survived—we have built our lives on what we needed to do: sell fruit, meats, goods, dance and sing for a living. I'm coming to you to tell you that I tried to be happy, but the cancer was my enemy. The enemy or death as some people call it, takes your physical life, but not your soul! I am glad that my family is carrying on with the reggae music. I wrote your favorite song when I was at my lowest depression. Our tradition usually puts family first, but not always. I had a few wives and girlfriends, and lots of children. My love I wanted to spread around, like the birds with the flowers, ya know. I wanted to spread my joy to many people. They might call me a saint now because I gave my gift back, but I'm not a saint—I'm just someone who got noticed. I never liked food—honest—I liked my smokes first as the Rastafarians do.

I see you, Michele, and I know you as a gifted artist, and I understand you. The highs and lows of your personality—your creativity. And I know the rhythms or beat of music is most important for people to hear. People see, they hear and they feel. People that can no longer feel, or see through emotional hard times, can still hear. So a performer who plays music and sings brings them pleasure while they hear the performance. But I must say as I'm sittin' here that I think music is the most important thing in the world. So you've got to love what you do, for yourself and then give this gift out to the world. Michele, you can't sing, but you can paint, can perform and you can write. It's good when people can see the truth, when they can read about it, and people will then think about what they're reading!

So I popped by to say "Hey Mon" and to tell you that in this world, which you call Heaven, I'm still creating music. I also help inspire those musicians on earth to find joy in their lives. I was the "King of Reggae" they called me, but I was not the first to bring joy with music, or I'm not the last. Over here there are places to go, where we can look down to see people in your world and help them. So I'm a teacher, which is a good thing, as teachers are important here—just like music is. I guide and help inspire some songwriters and performers on earth too. I wanted to say "Irie"—all is well. I wanted to tell you that your work is important. I'm just your friend saying hello. Have a good trip and relax. That's all I have to say for now.

PS: At the beginning of our dissertation, he told me that I would hear my favorite song of his very soon, and it would be a validation for me that he communicated. About an hour later, while we were relaxing on Negril Beach, a musician and composer came by. We realized that he was the one who played at our "wedding vows" renewal celebration the year before in 2013. He didn't seem to recognize us wearing our sunglasses, hats and cover-ups. He was playing his new composition and when he played his guitar, he swung his dreadlocks. When the musician was starting to walk away he turned, smiled and played my favorite song—the one the Reggae King told me I would soon hear! When we motioned him over he recognized us and told us about his new composition, called "Come to Negril," which he then played for us. I'm sure the "King of Reggae" was guiding him! When a spirit tells me that a confirmation is coming, it always does.

7

The Soul Review

Over the years, many of my clients who came for consultations later became friends. Judy was one of them. She was divorced, and I adored her little daughter. At that time I had created a series of unicorn prints from my original paintings and gave some of the prints to her daughter, Samantha, who treasured them. I passed along some of my clothes to Judy, and we even took her daughter to Disney's Ice Capades one year. Judy had a government job, but she was always drawn to alternate ways of healing. She took me to a Chinese acupuncturist a few times, and she enjoyed attending some of the Mind Body Spirit Expos where I presented.

I later learned that Judy had developed colon cancer. She was in her mid-50s and had never had a colonoscopy. She passed away shortly after her cancer diagnosis. I missed her friendship and our spiritual chats, and stayed in touch with her daughter. Then on one occasion after meditating, I saw the spirit of Judy sitting in front of me, wearing a big grin. She briefly shared her ideas about a "soul review," reincarnation and training to be spirit guides. The following is Judy's story:

Soul Review

Hi, I want to tell you about a process that is similar to the life review after death. It is an assessment of your past lives and is called a "soul review." The life review enables you to see the last life you just left behind and what you accomplished for spiritual growth. The soul review is for you to witness *many* past lives and how they affected other people, as well as yourself. It is a hologram that is created that stores all of your thoughts, decisions and experiences. Some call it a personal "Hall of Records" and some call it the Akashic Records. I see now that you are capable of accessing the "Akashic Records" for your clients, and that pleases me. I wish you could have done that for me while I was living on earth. We can't go back and relive our lives again, but we can access past lives to evaluate our spiritual progress.

I was a Native American Indian in a past life (which you briefly told me about), and when I reviewed that lifetime, I was pleased! My love of nature and animals, my compassion and loyalty stem from that one lifetime in the West. I was also drawn, as you know, to natural ways of healing. My pull towards the homeopathic approach (using herbs and oils) came from my lifetime as an assistant to a shaman healer.

I'm in great peace now, and I need to tell you not to worry about things. As you know, worry brings on stress and stress can affect the physical body. I just couldn't handle the fighting, the bickering and financial problems of my recent past life.

When I was fully able to access the Akashic Records of my last 110 lifetimes, I saw my progression in a new way. I also learned that I soul contracted to be a healer this past lifetime but fell short of the mark because stress and worry held me back. I saw how worry only produces more negativity, which I feel led to my cancer. Stress is toxic to the body. I now value the saying, "go with the flow." How free everything is on this side. There is no time here, so we can spend many years (in your earth time) studying, learning, teaching and training to be spirit guides for those on earth. We do not need to be relatives of the people that we want to help. I've had Asian lifetimes involved with acupuncture, and I can even train to be a spirit guide helper for those now practicing acupuncture on earth. So everyone on earth has spirit guides. Guides can help with certain projects that a person is involved with and then retract from earth and work on something else over on this side.

Reincarnation

Another possibility that I want to talk about is that your soul is capable of going back to a past time in history. Your soul can re-incarnate back to bring something of value to the world. Most people think of reincarnation as a process of moving ahead into the future. But I've learned that souls can study here and take that advanced information back to the past in earth history. There is a belief called *paradox* where scientists say that it's impossible to go back in time. But an advanced soul can choose to do this. The process is usually done in only one incarnation, to help the progression of society. The concept of going back in time deals with inventions, the arts or science. Einstein incarnated here from our future, to bring advanced information through about the theory of relativity. So did Leonardo da Vinci, who was a pioneer of inventions and the arts, along with Tesla and others. We can incarnate back into a past time frame or ahead into a future one. Going back in time only applies to very advanced souls, who will change the course of history in a positive, enlightened way.

I would like to go back in time to the American Indian days with the knowledge I have now, before the "white man" (as we called him) entered the picture. Nature provided everything for us then. We ate meat, berries, herbs and natural things from Mother Earth. We were happy during our ceremonies and very peaceful, spiritual people. Even though a tribe may have fought against another tribe at times, that is the only stress we had. But I know I can only go back to that time period if I have something of great value to give.

Spirits here that merge with Universal Knowledge spend much time reviewing their past lives for soul growth and evaluation. That assessment helps them to decide where and when they want to reincarnate for advancement. The pinnacle of soul growth is for those who have obtained pure compassion, humility, integrity and love of society. Therefore they do not need to reincarnate again. When souls have reached the status of purity (meaning soul enlightenment), they become "ascended master teachers."

Teachers are very well respected on this side. There are souls who choose not to reincarnate to earth ever again, but study with ascended beings here who teach them about compassion and other virtues. But the fastest way to advance is to incarnate into dire situations, so that you can learn from them. Those souls who choose autism, physical disabilities, severely dysfunctional families and poverty do so to rapidly progress. By choosing disabilities or challenging situations, they can better learn patience and tolerance, or they can teach their family strength, forgiveness or faith. Feel empathy towards people in these situations, but do not pity them, for they have chosen these conditions for advancement.

We forget all of this knowledge when we take our first breath as a baby, so that our path is clear and clean to enable us to start over again.

I wanted you to know and understand the soul review of past lives that we have access to. And to confirm that each individual soul has their own Hall of Records called the "Akasha." These personal records can only be accessed with permission from that particular soul. If another soul (or a person on earth) wants to obtain knowledge from another's Hall of Records, they need consent to do so! If one of our own spirit guides needs to access our records to help us choose a future life, they can do so only with our permission. The records are private for each individual soul to review, and only those others with the highest intentions and permission can obtain information from them.

I hope this is of interest to you,

Judy

8

Becoming Spirit Guides

It was a late afternoon in August, and I was relaxing on my upper deck above the sunroom. While I was sipping iced tea at the patio table, I looked up and saw the spirit of a gentleman sitting across from me. He projected as a light-skinned, African-American with a charming smile and a seemingly kind demeanor. I ran into my adjoining office to obtain pen and paper. This was the telepathic message I received:

Hello, my name is Ralph, and my happiest times were during the 1940s in Chicago, Illinois. I was a butcher then and a good provider for my family. The Army didn't draft me because I had flat feet (he chuckles). I had a precious wife Mary, and two daughters—Rose and Lillian. Lillian was my mother's name, and that's who my firstborn daughter was named after. Rose was the baby, and she was always my "baby girl."

My day consisted of getting up around 5 AM, drinkin' a cup of coffee and then goin' down to the butcher shop with lunch at noon and dinner at 5. Our family lived right above the shop, and the buildin' was three stories high. I had two employees at that time and was proud to say that as black folks in those days, we rarely owned a business. One was my brother Paul, Jr. and my other employee was my good friend Bill.

It was a life of simplicity and freedom. I heard stories 'bout my African ancestors comin' here to America as slaves. Some were horror stories, but I seemed to break the mold of dark times when I started my first job in that very butcher shop in 1914. I was born in 1902, and then kids would either go to school or work. I never had *schoolin'* as we called it, but I did learn to read and write. The old white man who ran the shop took a great likin' to me. I was a good kid and tried hard to please.

I was brought up to be honest. "A penny saved is a penny earned," the old man would say. So I started savin'. By the time I was 22 I had saved a good amount, enough to get married to my beautiful wife. Her dad worked on the railroad and liked me. I was the only boy she ever dated with some money (Ralph laughs).

The old butcher, McGreever, left me the business in his will, which was unheard of in those days (long before civil rights). I stayed outta trouble, and my wife and I moved upstairs into the third floor to take care of Mrs. McGreever who was ailin'. There my first daughter, Lily, was conceived and born, and two years later little Rose. I always felt there were angels watchin' over us. There were fires in different parts of Chicago then, but they never came to us. There was a lota crime, but we were never robbed or hurt. When McGreever's widow passed away, we moved in for good and made it our forever home. The couple never had any children, so there were no relatives of theirs to give us trouble.

It was a great life; I had no complaints. Our shop was one of the main meat shops in the city, supplyin' mainly restaurants. We had a freezer section in the back, but all meat was only held for two days. It was always fresh. My girls didn't like the shop—that was a man's world.

Well anyhow, I died of a heart attack when I was 50 years old in the shop while my friend, Bill, was there. The rest of my family was at church for a prayer meetin'. When they got home, they got the news that I had passed away. After I died, my wife never remarried. My daughter Lily was six months pregnant with her first baby at the time. Her husband was a good man and came to work at the butcher shop. So now I'll tell you my story, about Heaven, the one I want you to hear.

Spirit Guide Training

I went to Heaven, through the tunnel, just like others have said. When I got to this bright light, there was a little boy waitin', holdin' hands with my grandpa (my dad's father). I didn't know who this little boy was at first, but he said, "Grandpa" and ran to me. Then I figured this was the soul of Lily's son who was about to be born. I didn't see my own dad right away in Heaven, just those two. After my book of life review I was asked what I wanted to do next. My grandbaby boy was goin' down to earth in three months, and I wanted to watch over him. Then a spirit helper came to me and said, "Ralph, do you want to train to be a helper of your grandson? He's from your soul group here, and you've been with him before in past times." Yes, I felt an instant love when I saw my grandson standin' there again like I knew him forever (Ralph chuckles again).

I said to the spirit helper, "Sure thing, I wanna watch over him always." After that we went to an area that looked like a big office. There were souls lookin' pretty serious as they went through files. Then there appeared a big movie screen, but different from the screen in my life review. This screen was to view things that *could* happen in my grandson's future life! There we stood, my grandson and me, viewing his life—from his first breath to his last. I saw his upcomin' trials against racial prejudices. I saw his pull towards alcohol. I saw his loneliness and his possible triumphs and successes. He had already chosen to learn tolerance against racial prejudice. So he was not gonna have the easy life I had. He would need a lovin' "spirit guide" (they called it) to gently help him along his path—to guide, support and influence his development (they said).

My grandson had free choice as we all do, and his final decisions I could not stop. But to help with things for his highest good, I could do. Then he left me because he was goin' down to earth. In his case a place of violence and hardship, for this is the soul lesson he chose. It took him courage to pick this life and be born to my daughter, Lillian. I was proud that they named him Ralph the third! My grandpa was also named Ralph, who met me at the tunnel with little Ralph, my grandson.

So I'd check in every few weeks in your earth time to see how my grandson was doin'. He was my focus for a while in Heaven, until he joined me again and remembered who I was. You see, we forget when we are born on earth. We have to forget to have free will and make our own decisions. A "spirit guide" is a lovin' human soul helper, who in Heaven makes you the main focus of their existence. Each one of you on earth has a couple lifetime spirit guides. Some are from your soul group in Heaven and some are not. They watch and help you to learn 'bout the "soul lesson" you picked. So as they give you their lovin' energy, they learn from you too.

I didn't want or need to be born to learn about racial prejudice. I learned the pitfalls of it by helpin' my grandson. We can learn on earth and we can also learn in Heaven. Now, most of our family from Chicago has joined me here. Although we're family, some of them are off workin', teachin', learnin' or creatin'. And so it is.

It was an honor and a token of love to serve as a spirit guide for my beloved grandson.

Thank you kindly for listenin',

Ralph

The next story is from another interesting male spirit who communicated with me and whom I had never met. He relayed compelling information about his lifetime in India, and how he and his wife have chosen to become spirit guides:

My name is Pujan. I am a Hindu from India. I was a tradesman while on earth. I traded goods like tea, jewelry and beads, fine silk and embroidered cloth to those in England. Our family did not trade opium. I lived from 1892 until 1914. My father was a tradesman, and I learned the work from him. I lived a modest life and died rather young from an intestinal parasite. The new big ships would travel to India from England for our goods. Ivory was another commodity for the Englishmen to carve and make jewelry and trinkets with. We revered the elephant as a deity, but poachers would kill them for their tusks. My father and I did not buy ivory from the poachers, but a friend of my father who was quite poor would bring us the ivory. It was wrong to sell such things, but my father's compassion for his friend led him to buy the ivory to help him out.

I am coming to you to tell you that we can create Hindu temples in this dimension. Some from India have retained cultures and traditions here and do not wish to immediately enter into the universal consciousness as one energy. All human souls experience a life review. I was in love with a 15-year-old girl named Dhara. It was not unusual to marry girls from age 12 on. We were married when she was 15, which was rather old for a girl in our society. I was 17. Dhara was a good wife and beautiful. She would weave designs in silk and we would sell the silk to the tradesmen from England. There were no machines then to embroider or make designs. Therefore my wife would be considered quite an artist. She worked many long hours. Silk came to us from the silkworm in Asia. It was tan in color. My wife would die the pieces, then draw designs on them and embroider them with gold and silver thread. This process was time-consuming and laborious, but we got good money for them. Dhara was not a seamstress, so she did not make jackets or skirts, just long scarves.

We took our religion of Hinduism seriously and revered the deities like Ganesh. We had a son when she was 16 and I was 18. We named him Pujan as the name was handed down. I loved him dearly and he would always be next to my wife when she created her scarves. A ship would come to port about every other month, so there was time to gather our wears to trade. Herbal tea was most popular along with spices.

I want to give you my background so I can explain how I died and how my soul left my body. We believed in reincarnation, but I have not reincarnated for 100 years in your earth time. I waited for my wife and son to join me. Our family unit was very strong, and I had no desire to enter earth again until I met up with them here. Even now my wife and son are still with me. We have retained the Hindu ways because we want to, not because we have to of course.

My wife has chosen to be a spirit guide of three artists now living on earth. One artist resides in India and two live in America. The artist in India is working with textiles and designing clothing, which is sold in American boutiques. The two others that she helps in America are painters and employ the technique of ancient Indian art with the same symbols and colors. Although her spirit may come down to earth to visit our family that has evolved through generations, Dhara loves her art and loves to help and guide these three people on earth. She helps by inspiring and influencing creative ideas. So spirit guides, as you call them, do not necessarily choose to help family members. This is important for you to hear. Some people living on earth know of their spirit guides and some do not.

There is only light here and no time, no pain, no prejudice. My uncle (my father's brother) has already reincarnated in America but still holds interest in all things from India. But for us this is sheer heaven, to be here and together as a family.

Next I want to tell you about my death. At age 22 one day I felt sick and dizzy. I was walking down the dirt street in our town, and it was very busy at that hour and overpopulated as many towns are in India. I fell over with a stomach cramp and was carried home. Another uncle (not the one I mentioned before) was a healer who worked with herbs and natural remedies. Ginger was good for the stomach and cinnamon for blood. He made me drink teas with herbs and spices, but I had a fever and did not get better. I had an intestinal parasite from food I ate from the Englishmen, which caused a bleeding stomach ulcer. I was also hemorrhaging and very weak. My wife was very upset, and she gave our son to the relatives to keep for a while. I lay in bed, on my cot for a week in great pain. Hindu prayers were said and offerings were given to our deities, but it was my time to leave. I did not want to leave, but I soul contracted a young age to die. I first had to bring my son into the world.

My son was my brother in a past life in a part of Africa which was very primitive. We both agreed to incarnate at the same time to learn the ways of India. I did not realize at the time we made this agreement how much I would love that country. The deities like Shiva or Kali are as real to us as your Jesus is real to you. Therefore they exist in Heaven because we believe they do!

When I died I left my body and floated up to the ceiling. I saw my wife crying, and my family gathered around me. Even at this point I did not want to leave but had to honor my agreement. My body was later cleansed, wrapped and burned, but I did not want to see that part. As I ascended through a portal, I saw souls wandering around. They seemed confused. I saw their "light bodies" but could not tell what nationality they were. I did not see clothes on them, and they were even walking *through* each other! I later learned that some of these souls did not realize they were dead and were confused. I wanted to leave that realm because as you would say in America, they were like walking zombies.

As I went higher in the astral world I saw a blue color; it was the most beautiful and clear shade. A spirit of a man came toward me who I did not recognize. He merely said, "I am Omar, your helper." I later learned he was a guide who was helping me to learn compassion in that lifetime in India. My father showed compassion to his poor friend by buying ivory, even though my father knew it was wrong to sell parts from our sacred animals. I learned compassion with the love I saw in my wife's eyes when she held our newborn son. So at age 22, my lesson for that lifetime had been gained, and Omar helped to open my eyes to see this lesson.

Although it may seem strange, I never had a lifetime with Omar. So my point is that spirit guides do not have to be relatives or necessarily have had past incarnations with us. Our people from India, whether they practice yoga or not, are very conscious of balancing mind, body and spirit. The art of meditation is done to achieve this.

I wanted to contact you because you did not know me on earth, and we have never met. I heard about your project on writing about Heaven and wanted to share my experience. Heaven is what we make of it. It is a composite of our beliefs and the things we love. I have had a total of 240 lifetimes on earth and of those my last lifetime in India was my favorite. There I learned my soul lessons quickly, loved and learned about compassion and had to leave at age 22 to fulfill my soul contract.

I am very interested in the stock market in America and how people are trading commodities and goods. I myself have trained to help a couple people in the US who are doing this. So my point is we do not have to incarnate to do good; we can become spirit guides and help others from here who still are alive on earth. The concept of spirit guides needed to be addressed I thought.

As I have stated, I, my wife and my son do not wish to return to earth. We have decided to stay in this realm for a long time. We do not have 9 a.m. to 5 p.m. workdays, and we can go to viewing stations to see how our projects and earth people are progressing. Then my wife and I can meet up and telepathically talk about the progress of the people on earth we have chosen to help.

This is my story and my experience. I hope you will find this interesting for your book.

Namasté,

Pujan

9

Meeting Jesus

Today I sit across from the lovely spirit of a lady. A lady I knew well in life, though I'm a little surprised that she wants to converse now. Daisy was an African-American who was very religious but also spiritual. When I say spiritual, the "Spirit of God" was in her heart. She was a homeopathic healer, had the gift of "laying on of hands," and did hydrotherapy (colon cleansing). A very well-known "born again" evangelist in Oklahoma heard of her abilities, and she was called there to heal his wife. Her healing reputation spread, and yet she remained very humble. Daisy believed in my work and my ability to talk to those in Heaven. On one of my visits to her clinic, I received accurate information from her departed husband and mother. Later, after she passed away, Daisy gave me messages to share with her remaining daughter. I count her as a friend and as a beautiful soul:

Hello Michele, this is Daisy. I'm glad to converse with you and want you to know how happy I am in Heaven! I've met up with all of my relatives and my dear husband. I see from here that you are helping many to heal from loss and that is a wonderful thing. I'd like to share my experience of crossing over.

My tunnel was amethyst purple in color with many vibrant royal blue sparkles. Jesus was the first being I saw. He gently said, "Welcome home." Jesus took me to a garden filled with yellow and pink roses and we sat together on a charming bench. I felt very comfortable there. Then down the garden path to greet me walked my mother, my grandparents and my husband. These were the loved ones that I was the closest to while living on earth, and I was so delighted to see them. Jesus and my family asked me to follow them, and they took me to a vast green meadow. There was a picnic area created for me and many from my soul group in Heaven were waiting there. We had a family reunion, and although we could no longer eat, there was a huge table with all of the southern food that I remembered. What a reunion we had as we reminisced about the past. In the distance I heard my favorite hymns being sung by an angelic choir. It was a safe, joyful and peaceful setting.

I learned that true unconditional love exists on earth and here in Heaven. People are not condemned for their religious beliefs. God, who is pure love, accepts all souls who have love in their hearts, regardless of their beliefs. We have physical bodies on earth, while here we have our "soul bodies." There is nothing negative or dark here, all is bright glistening light.

After I had experienced my book of life review, I was asked how I wanted to progress. I chose to study the ways of my Master, Jesus, and learn how He healed with perfect love. There are many ascended teachers in Heaven that souls can study with. We are never forced to learn or to help other souls to progress, but we can choose to. Since there is no time here, it seems like I just arrived in the blink of an eye. Churches, cathedrals and synagogues are created here where souls can pray or meditate. We are one with God and in total bliss.

I only have my own perspective to share. I guess there are different layers of energy here but I am not familiar with the lower regions. I pray that those in the lower gray, desolate space can learn about love and the light of God. Prayer is a powerful thing. We can pray for souls here in Heaven or for those people still on earth.

Keeping things simple is what I choose to do now, learning more about natural ways of healing, praying for others, attending a church with my relatives, listening to choirs of singers and studying with the Master, Christ.

We do create our own heavens, and for now this is mine.

Thank you,
Love and light,
Daisy

10

From Comatose to Beyond

In the early 1990s, we would have spiritual get-togethers in our local metaphysical community. These spiritual meetings were very enlightening, and there I met a special person named Carol. In addition to being instrumental in organizing these get-togethers, she was a psychiatric nurse, Reiki master and certified hypnotherapist. She brought much to the table with her wise counseling. We shared many personal stories over the years and became very close.

In 2012, during surgery, Carol lapsed into a coma and did not regain consciousness. Her daughters contacted me to see if I could derive any messages from her in that condition. She did have a living will, but her girls wanted some kind of closure before they pulled the plug.

I went to visit Carol in the hospital and had everyone clear the room. The last physical sense to be diminished is hearing, so I talked softly to Carol while holding her pale, lifeless looking hand. I glanced up, and above her physical body was her "light body" hovering on the ceiling! Then I closed my eyes, and when I opened them, her soul was calmly sitting in the chair by the hospital window.

I came prepared to write down information in case she would communicate in her comatose state and received three pages of conversation from her for her family. The last thought she telepathically sent to me was, "Tell my girls I have my hair done to go to Heaven." This information was greatly appreciated, and that afternoon they courageously took her off life support. Her daughters later told me that before surgery she insisted on getting her hair done as she did every week.

It didn't surprise me that she would come through to me when I started writing this book. Carol gave valuable details on what it was like for her to be in a comatose state and what we may expect on the other side. She mentioned the life review that we all experience and explained about viewing stations where souls can see their loved ones still on earth. It was also confirmed that our earthly beliefs, whether religious or otherwise, can carry over and be re-created in the next world. The following is Carol's story:

Comatose State

First, I'm fine, have arrived over here and already I'm making new friends. I was ready to leave my body, tired physically and losing hope. I need to say that *here* is amazing. It is a world of thought forms created by energy. I was relieved that you came to the hospital to help me cross over while on life support. I did *hear* you and actually my soul *saw* you when I was out of my body, looking down. You encouraged my daughter's (I call them "my girls"), to let me go. I didn't want to lie there and be nothing or do nothing. I think people should let their family members die with dignity and not artificially keep them alive. We soul contract a timeline to learn lessons, and when that is complete the soul wishes to go.

When in a coma the soul travels back and forth from earth to Heaven. But the soul cannot fully enjoy the light in Heaven because the light body is still attached to the physical body by an invisible cord. This cord is located at the abdomen, where the umbilical cord was attached. We all astral travel on certain nights while sleeping, which means our souls can leave our bodies to do spiritual work. But we return via the invisible "silver cord" still attached to the navel region. When a baby is born, the umbilical cord is cut. The soul cord is severed *only* when the soul leaves the body upon death. I believe that keeping someone artificially alive is like trying to shove a newborn back into the womb and not cut the umbilical cord! It's quite unnatural.

When a person passes away that spiritual cord is severed, leaving the physical body behind and the soul free to soar to Heaven. It is like the analogy of the butterfly—the cocoon being the body and the butterfly representing the soul that flies free. When the butterfly is ready to make the transition to leave its cocoon and fly, it does. Now can you imagine NOT letting the butterfly emerge when it is time? Can you imagine the torment the butterfly would feel by not being able to emerge to the next state of being? For me, that is what it was like being trapped in a physical body while in a coma.

A soul's timeline to pass away is agreed upon even before birth, and yet there is no completion to a life while in a comatose state. In this condition a soul has one foot here in Heaven and one still on earth. It's like a perpetual near-death experience. The soul can float down the hospital hallway and even visit other people's souls who are in a coma. Today there is a lot of emphasis on the paranormal and earthbound spirits still residing on battlefields and in historic buildings. But you'll actually find more paranormal activity in the hospital wing that houses comatose patients than about anywhere else on earth! While in a coma the light body waits and waits to be set free from the physical body. In fact it can be a little torturous for a human soul to endure.

Again, when I was in a coma I could leave my body at will, float to the ceiling of the hospital room and astrally travel down the hall. But it was a sad experience for me because I wasn't fully free. I couldn't totally let go.

I feel other people on artificial life support experience the same feelings. They can hear others on earth speak to them but cannot converse. If they could, they might tell you to let them go! Individual souls can actually choose a coma situation. This decision is not a conscious one, but a soul-mind decision. And it is not to test their loved ones on earth, but to instill courage in them as they sever the life support cord.

So tell your readers not to have guilt if they have had a relative on sustained artificial life support. We are not taught or awakened to the process of dying. The only thing that dies is the physical body and brain. The *true* part of a person is the soul and mind, which is energy and which is eternal. By being in the comatose state myself I truly now understand it.

Although a person in a coma longs to go to the light and move on with their soul's evolution, it's sometimes blocked by family members who are not educated to the process of letting go. I know that there is a lot of emotional anguish when a family finally decides to "pull the plug." And of course some of this stigma is also founded in religion. Some believe in the idea of a physical body eventually rising intact, ascending into Heaven and getting on with things. However, this place we call our true home is not a physical world. It is a place of light, love and spiritual beauty.

I also want to add that there are cases where people do regain consciousness and awaken from the comatose state. In those cases the soul of the person chooses to return. Even though their timeline may be up, the soul may grow tired of being in limbo caused by artificial life support and the energy of the family clinging to them. Since we have free choice, the soul may choose to return to the physical body for a few more years.

But I was so happy when my girls freed me from that prison or physical tomb, and this is what happened to me after I was freed:

Transition

After my soul finally left my body, I floated up and forward at a fairly rapid speed. I intuitively knew what to expect, so I wasn't afraid. The tunnel seemed like a spiral as I was thrust through it. I know the soul experiences that connecting portal at physical birth, while being pushed down through the birth canal, but returning home to the Universal Mind of God is very quick, and then you enter another world—Heaven.

We have returned to Heaven many times before, but at first we forget that we have. Just as a soul entering a new baby body on earth has a form of amnesia, the same experience happens when we re-enter this world. But then the memories return. Not only do relatives and pets appear that we have loved, but members from our soul group, some of which have not incarnated with us in the lifetime we just left. But when you see them you *remember*—you are awakened to the light.

The soul reunion can last a long time in earthly measure. As was stated before, there is no time here as you know it on earth. So we may stay in a greeting and reunion mode for even a couple of years. Then the guides come—those who are our mentors. They form a council, not to judge us, but for us to be objective in our life review.

Life Review

The life review is mentioned by some who have had a near-death experience (NDE). The longer a person is pronounced clinically dead, the more time the soul has to reach their life review. When I met with my "council," a few were ascended guides. One guide took a Native American Indian form as he was an ancient wise one. Another guide took the form of St. Germaine, clothed in purple and emanating golden light. And still another looked similar to Jesus, wearing a robe and sandals. When I saw them, I knew them and remembered them. They helped and influenced my welfare while I was on earth; I just didn't remember that while in my physical body. All in all there were 12 in my council. They said in unison, "Are you ready?" I remembered then that they were referring to the review of the life I had just left.

An area is created for you to review your earthly life's journey. There is no space in this realm so a place must be created. This is achieved by "thought forms" from the council's soul minds. My review area was plain with a large wooden bench to sit on. In front of me was a screen that also stretched around me, so I was in the "center" of my life review. It was like viewing a hologram or a three-dimensional movie.

I saw my mother giving birth to me along with every detail from my first to my last breath on earth. I again felt feelings of love, fear, hurt and ecstasy. I viewed myself in joy and in tears. The experience was not just about my own feelings, but also included those around me and how they felt. I could feel their *painful* emotions if I hurt them, and their *joy* when I was kind and loved them. The complete range of emotions that you can feel in the physical body, I could still feel in my spirit.

I remembered that we soul contract a purpose, a plan and a mission before each incarnation. My mission for my last lifetime was to learn patience and understanding, and to not be judgmental in any way. At times I fell short with patience, but stayed strong in trying to understand people. Being a trained psychiatric nurse gave me the ability to look deeper into others' lives. My profession also helped me with being nonjudgmental and objective in dealing with others. People may have thought that I had a cold personality because I was not expressive or dramatic. But I now gratefully realize that most of the lessons that I had soul contracted were obtained.

After this review of total understanding and feeling, I was asked a few questions by my Council of Guides. Was I happy with the life I just lived and was it fulfilling for me? What weaknesses in myself did I observe in my review and what strengths? Did I show overall love and compassion for my fellow humans? I thought about these questions and felt I had been pretty much on target. I stayed focused to my original soul agreement.

Then I was free to leave and do or create whatever I wanted. I immediately wanted to rest and meditate. As was stated we have no need for sleep here, but meditation is key. Spiritual meditation means we rest in the love of the Creator. There is no beginning or end here. This is a world of infinity.

The Soul Mind

Many question what's beyond. Although some have had a near-death experience, there are still scientists and doctors who believe that it's lack of oxygen to the brain cells that creates these visions. Well, the brain is one thing in the physical body, but the "soul mind" is another. I like the way you state in your lectures, Michele, that the human soul retains a mind, personality, memory bank and consciousness. All are true—energy cannot be destroyed, energy just takes on a different form.

Remember the example of water. At room temperature it flows, when frozen it becomes a solid form and when heated to boiling water creates steam or vapor. Yet it remains water. So the human soul inhabiting a body can also become different in form. In other words the soul enters as a light body at birth, but can leave and astral travel at night during sleep. And when the soul leaves upon death, it is in its purest form. It is totally free and unencumbered by the physical body, and then can create an environment with its soul mind.

I knew from experience that when you channel, Michele, a spirit can *project* the way it wants to look. That projection of the soul's energy is created by the soul's mind. The individual mind is the most powerful thing in the universe. The mind can make the physical body ill when it is stressed, which means out of balance, negative or confused. The mind can also create abundance and perfect health! And here in this world we can immediately create our own environments with our soul minds. That is astounding!

Creating Environments

The creative Universal Mind that we call God is love. It is comprised of pure positive thought forms. The mind of

God will not and cannot stand for anything dark or negative. Yes, there are polarities of light and darkness on earth, and there needs to be for balance. But when we transition to another form of pure light, we return to the source of unconditional love. When we are united with Universal Mind we can create anything, in any form. With focus we can do this physically on earth (there is the "Law of Attraction"), but extensively through our soul mind here in this dimension. Yes, this is a world of individual creation and there are no limitations.

We retain our earthly belief systems when we arrive here. So it is true that if someone has lived a peaceful Buddhist life they will expect to see Buddha and they do. Protestants may see Jesus, Catholics the Blessed Mother Mary and the saints, and so on. A handful of people who have had a near-death experience say they have seen the fires of hell. Before this happened they were probably ingrained to believe they were bad and were filled with fear. But this is a charade. Through this process the longer they remain with the Universal Mind of God, the more they realize there is no room for fear. Then they will awaken to the truth.

All man-made religions are good to a point because they keep a semblance of order in society. They are based on the teachings of ascended masters. These masters of love and light taught about compassion—the Golden Rule in each religion. But humans on earth translated these teachings in different ways, most written hundreds of years after the ascended one had returned to Heaven. Religion does inspire goodness, but can also promote fear. Here we create our own environments with our soul minds, therefore each individual creates their own Heaven.

There is no need for verbal communication here because we work in a telepathic manner. We can share memories with other souls by formulating pictures of events and sending them directly to their minds. Of course we have no tears, fears or distress. Since we create our own Heavens, each soul will visualize a pleasing environment. A soul may create a kitchen with their reunited relatives; some will create beautiful streams and meadows; while others create mansions or simple dwellings.

We can remember the taste and smell of food and drink and can re-create these senses, but those desires are fleeting. We are HOME, our true home, and have no need of any material aspects. It is fun to remember that thoughts create things, and we can create for as long as we want! If souls, for example, still feel comfortable going to church to pray they can create a church, cathedral or synagogue. Or if they wish to study, they can visit universities of learning which have been telepathically created by educated geniuses. There are as many things to do here spiritually as there are to do physically on earth.

This is a place of higher frequency in which we are one with the Creator and indeed create our own environments with our thought forms. So whether they are forests, mountains, lakes, the ocean or gardens, all are created from our memory banks and are pleasurable for us. Even a favorite reclining chair in a special room that you remember can be formulated. We do retain our mind, our memories and our personalities. So "creating" is a wonderful ability here.

At first I created a nature scene with rocks and a waterfall to enable me to sit and meditate. But since I enjoyed working with people as a counselor and healer on earth, counseling is the work that I've *chosen* to do now. Some souls actually need a form of rehab. They have *forgotten* that they came from love and beauty. They have *forgotten* that they are special, wonderful and unique creations of God. They have *forgotten* the spiritual ways of the soul journey. This is when they come to me, Michele. As you awaken others to spiritual truths on earth, I awaken souls to the spiritual truths *here* that have been long forgotten!

Viewing Stations

I also want to explain the concept of viewing stations. These stations are created for spirits to see how their loved ones are doing on earth. We can lower our frequencies and walk through a connecting portal to the earth plane if we choose to touch those we still love. It's essentially like walking from a higher room down to a lower one. But there are souls who do not wish to walk through the portal to be close to those remaining on earth. They prefer to view them like a three-dimensional movie.

If for example (in viewing stations) we see our children crying and in distress because of illness or emotional pain, we may long to help them by pulling our "soul energy" down for assistance. While other souls may just choose to send goodwill and prayers down for their loved ones welfare without being compelled to enter the earth plane. It is up to the individual soul how to proceed. The viewing stations keep us connected to those we love on earth by being able to see their welfare. There are situations where souls are compelled to view family members—on their birthdays, on holidays, and other special occasions or if they are ill.

Soul Essence

In this dimension we also can meet and learn with scholars like Einstein, inventors like Tesla, musicians like Mozart or artists like Rembrandt. Remember that the light body is mutable energy, it can divide or splinter off and be many places at once. Yes, in this realm part of your soul essence can take art lessons, while another part can be learning about science!

As a soul chooses to go back down to earth (the temporary home), the core of the person's soul always stays here. For example, think of an octopus. The head represents the core soul; the tentacles represent different parts of the soul essence that can be in different places at one time. The soul is expanded energy and not a finite singular being, like the physical body.

Summation

You on earth have the power to create what you desire and it's getting easier for everyone, as the veil is now thinning between worlds. You know it's important to be aware of your thoughts and guard them. It seems we all try to do good works and healing in the metaphysical community, but it's the *intention* of the motives that needs to be realized. There truly is a higher plan for everyone, a greater plan. Balance in all areas of a life is important.

From years of study I knew what to expect and I'm not disappointed. This side is a place of love. There is no purgatory or hell as some are taught. But there are different levels of energy here. The denser, lower gray areas are for younger souls who have committed horrific crimes, hurt many others and need to sleep or cocoon for awhile. The more advanced souls who were aware of kindness and forgiveness while on earth, immediately come to this frequency of light and are welcomed with open arms. By more advanced I mean they have progressed by learning empathy, compassion and love through many lifetimes on earth.

We are free to pursue any form of study. I loved rocks and minerals, and even though they are not physically here, I can learn about them with geologists who dedicated their lives to this form of study.

There are many ways to gain more insights. You can traverse back to the ancient wise teachers of yesteryear or move into the higher realm of ascended masters to learn more if you so choose.

Of course there is no religion, race, politics or prejudice. We are all free thinkers here and have the ability to explore new concepts of thought and reason. I know of some souls working in the science realm, while others are studying the arts, music and other creative endeavors.

And joyfully this realm is not all about work. As you have leisure time on earth we do here as well. We are not forced to learn, we choose to. Although souls do not need sleep to regenerate, as those on earth do, we can meditate or quiet our minds for renewal. There is no time as I have stated, so I can remain in a meditative state as long as desired. This stage of rest for me is quite satisfying.

Please understand that there is a higher plan for everyone, a greater plan. Strive to be kind to everyone. Balance in all areas of life is important. Let the ways of the world drop away and see beyond to what lies ahead. Live to the fullest while on Mother Earth and be among her people, but keep your mind and heart on higher things.

I count you as a friend. Thank you for sharing my experiences and blessings to you.

Carol

11

The Issue of Suicide

Suicide

Over the past couple of decades, many of my clients have questioned the act of suicide. Did a loved one who committed suicide go to hell? Are they in a safe place? Does God judge us for taking our own life? To obtain a greater perspective on this question, I communed with my own spirit guides and light beings. I learned that there can be many different scenarios and out comes involving this act.

A vast area is created for the arrival of suicide victims. There is no condemnation with the act of suicide; it is merely a choice, but the agreed-upon contract of a "timeline" for soul progression has been thwarted. God does love ALL of us. In the case of suicide it is the motivation behind the action that needs to be acknowledged. Did one take his or her life because of pain, depression or to save someone else's life; or was it an act of anger, revenge or to spite another person?

A mother jumping in front of an oncoming car to save her baby or a courageous soldier taking a bullet to protect another soldier are exhibits of valor. Then there are suicide situations like the World Trade Center attacks in New York City. There were cases of people jumping out of windows because of their own shock and the burning environment. Some people who commit suicide feel that their chosen life path is too difficult, so they premeditate the action and decide to end their misery. And still others are angry and commit the act out of revenge. What was the motivation behind the action? The intention behind any action always needs to be considered. No one is ever punished in the other realms of energy, but different circumstances will require different ways of healing and dealing with the act of suicide.

If a person lived an unselfish life and helped others, yet took their life due to pain, depression or despair, they still need to address their action. In their life reviews, all who take their lives will spiritually see the wake of mourning loved ones, and the devastation of those left behind on earth.

A soul may have contracted a longer life span to learn lessons and carry out a mission, yet cut their life short through a suicide. They may then decide to reincarnate sooner to make up for those lost years. Again we are never punished for anything we choose. However, if an individual soul contracted a life of 82 years to learn soul lessons and then took their life at 42, they have lost 40 years of development on earth. Certain souls will choose to immediately come back and live out those remaining years on earth, while others may work through it in a rehab situation in Heaven. Yes, there are advanced light bodies who counsel those who commit suicide, showing patience, love and guidance.

The negative part of suicide, then, is cutting a lifeline short and leaving an aftermath of grief for family and friends. A soul can never run away from the truth. The saying, "to thine own self be true," (from Shakespeare) is a valuable lesson for all.

On a late July afternoon in 2014, I was relaxing on our upper deck, directly above the sunroom where I usually work. When I glanced at the empty chair across from me, there sat the spirit of a lady. I did not recognize her as a friend, relative or client from this lifetime. I put a pen to paper and received this information from Marie, about her suicide and her life review. This communiqué really touched my heart, as it seemed to be simple and sincere. The following is her story:

My name is Marie. You don't know me and have never met me, but I know about you and your book project. (Marie wants to appear with dirty blonde looking hair, some wrinkles and a furrowed brow). I want to tell you how I made it out of the so-called "gray area;" how I went to rehab, forgave myself and others, and got through my life review.

I grew up in Iowa on a farm. My father sexually molested both me and my younger brother for many years when we were children. I did not have a pleasant or happy childhood. My mother was bipolar (a term you use today), but she was never diagnosed. She had mood swings and when our father was mean to us, she would look the other way.

I was born in 1958 and went to a school a few miles down the road. My brother and I walked to school, and we were very cold in the winter. My mother's name was Betty, and my dad was John. I know it will be difficult for you to sit there and hear what I have to say, but I must share it. I need to let people know that there is hope for all souls, no matter what they do on earth. When I say "hope," I mean there is love here on this side.

My brother got pneumonia when he was ten years old and died a year later because we didn't have the money for the doctor. My mother kept saying that he just had a cold. He would spit up blood and cry at night. We slept in the same bed, and I missed him so after he died. His name was Danny, after my paternal grandfather. I was not named after anyone, my mother said. She saw a black and white movie once and the actress's name was Marie.

So I ran away from home at 16 and hitchhiked my way to a nearby town. I had no money or clothes packed, but I couldn't stand the fighting and abuse at home. I wanted you to see me and how I looked around age 40, wrinkles and all. That's when I came to Heaven in 1998. But here, in the love and light, we eventually all look beautiful and young, around the age of 30.

I got a job at a local town hardware store with minimum pay. The owner's son took a liking to me when I was 17 and he was 22. I knew he drank, but I wanted a new life to live on my own. I had never heard about Jesus or love or even the word forgiveness. I didn't think much about the future, so I ran away with him. His dad disowned him, and we had no money. When we had some money, he'd buy liquor with it. So it was never a happy life for me.

I had a baby, a little girl, when I was 20. My husband's mother took pity on us and sent us money, knowing she now had a granddaughter. Her name was Sarah Jane, and she was beautiful. After Sarah Jane was born, I got even more depressed and felt alone. I was working as a housekeeper, cleaning and doing chores for people near our small house. My husband would not come home for a week sometimes, and I later learned his absence was from drinking.

I could have inherited my mother's mental condition, because I felt useless and had wild mood swings. Not wanting to hurt my daughter, I would sometimes leave her at one of the homes where I cleaned. The people there were older; they loved Sarah, and I almost thought they could be her grandparents. In a way they adopted her, since she was there almost every day after school. They gave me extra money too, especially at Christmas. My husband ran away with another woman and never returned. I felt sorry for Sarah, never knowing her dad, but it was probably better that way.

With every year that passed I felt more tired, more hopeless and more scared. In June of 1998, I went to the shed of one of my cleaning customers. They kept guns there to use for hunting. Guess I didn't think about it or plan it, but I just took a loaded gun, held it to my head and pulled the trigger. Thankfully this did not take place where Sarah was staying. The old gentleman had passed away by then and Sarah, who was now 20, was taking care of her surrogate grandma. Well, my spirit left my body, and I looked down at the horrible mess of myself that I left behind. Didn't know how I could look down at my body, since I no longer had eyes to see, but I saw! Also I didn't know what to do, 'cause nobody told me about what happens after death; I guess nobody knew about it. I saw the owner of the shed cover my body and clean up the mess. He was crying. There were horse stables nearby and I could float over to them, almost like flying, and see the horses. Well, I guess they could see me too, because they carried on so!

The old lady gave Sarah her house after I died and left the rest of her things to Sarah in her will. But I didn't know where to go or what to do. Guess you would call me an "earthbound" spirit. Finally, maybe about five years later in your earth time, I saw a being—the spirit of a man! He told me that he was from Heaven and chose to come down to get me, like a volunteer would do. He told me I had clung to earth long enough, and it was time to go with him. But he said I had "work" to do since I took my own life.

I was tired of working all of my earthly life and didn't want to go with him to do more work! Finally I agreed, since nobody could hear or see me anyhow. Only the animals could see me—the dogs, cats and horses. But I scared them because they would act up when they saw my essence.

So I first went to a place that was kind of gray and misty. There were no buildings or land, just a gray fog. I saw other beings walking around, back and forth, back and forth. Kind of like a caged lion I saw one time when the circus was in town. These spirits seemed lost and confused. The male spirit who came for me told me that they needed to go to a higher place; they needed to view their life over again. But most didn't want to relive their lives. A large number of these spirits took their lives; some were murdered or murdered others. I wandered around with them for a while, but it was lonely because nobody ever talked or smiled.

It took a lot of coaxing from the male volunteer spirit to get me out of there, but I felt ready. He telepathically told me not everyone who commits suicide or dies tragically comes here to this zone. Those who don't want to move on, who are angry, scared or confused come to this place. When I finally agreed to leave, we both seemed to rise higher and higher. Then I saw a light—a bright light that seemed to be everywhere. There were three spirits who came to me and said, "Welcome home, Marie. We're your spirit guides." I never met them when I was in my last life, but they knew me. They told me they couldn't stop me from killing myself because I had free choice, but they were happy that I made it this far.

The volunteer spirit who came down to the gray area to coax me to the light disappeared. It felt safe and peaceful in the light, and it was the very first time I had felt love (except from my daughter). Then I saw other spirits, and they hugged me and told me they were my ancestors.

I was taken to an area with a table that looked like half of a circle or a horseshoe. There sat other beings who called themselves "The Council." They talked to me about my life and what I thought of it, kind of like counselors would do. Then I was ready for my life review that I had to go through before I could totally move on.

Like a movie surrounding me, I first saw myself being born. My birth took place at my small shack of a home in the bedroom. My mother's sister was there to help. I watched as my soul actually entered my baby girl's body, and my life began! I relived every thought, emotion, experience—whether it was good or bad. There were so many people who had hurt me, but there were some who were kind to me. This review happened very quickly it seemed, until I got to the shed where the guns were. Then that scene was in slow motion. There were no thoughts of my daughter's welfare or who would find me or where my soul was going. I just wanted out, like a scared child, I wanted to run away.

As I watched my life movie, I regretted that last action on earth and never living to hold my grandchildren. I think the act of suicide is a selfish act, at least for me it was. I don't think all acts of suicide are selfish though. From that review, I understood everything and why I chose such a life of hardship. I chose that life to learn emotional strength and forgiveness, for that was my purpose. The council said it's not too late to forgive! So I was taken to another area where I viewed everyone who ever hurt me in that last lifetime. Some people were dead, while some were still living on earth. One by one, I told them that I forgave them, and that made me feel free and happy.

A number of spirits stay in the lower region called the gray area for a long time until they have the courage to move on. I had soul contracted a life of 68 years, but through my suicide had cut my agreement short.

Now I'm a volunteer in Heaven who goes to the lower level to help earthbound spirits like I was to get to the light. Not all suicides go to the gray area first; some come directly with me to the bright light and love of Heaven. By helping other souls I feel that I'm giving back to people in some way.

And that's my story. I pray it helps people to know that there is always hope, always love, always goodness somewhere. I learned that God is love, and God is everywhere.

Thank you,
Marie

The following communication is from a well-known actor and comedian. This gentleman took his life, and this is one of the last stories I received for my book. His story was about his suicide, with a different spin. I feel in essence that each individual on earth has a personal and unique way of crossing over. This dissertation reinforced that belief.

Hi, don't want to bother you, and I'm probably the last spirit you thought you'd hear from, but I'm here to discuss suicide. I took my life, and I did it because I was tired—plain and simple. I had lived my life in the limelight, always trying to make people happy, to make them laugh. I was, as you would call it, an "empath." I was able to actually "morph" into another person and become a different persona. I never thought I would be an actor or comedian when I was young. It just happened, and I guess you'd say "fate" pushed me and pushed me from one triumph to another. Although my performances seemed effortless, they were torture for me. I found myself either not grounded as to who I really was or totally grounded in another persona. As you yourself trance channel, I understand how draining it would be for you to take on another personality from the spirit world. I know it's difficult to be constantly changing personalities when the spirits come through you to speak. I understand the process; I can relate to you, and therefore want to help you with your book. You only have one other person who committed suicide to include in your book, and you probably would like to have another perspective on that action. Well, here I am!

I didn't mean to let my family down; I loved and still do love my kids. You call addictions "demons to bear," and I call them weaknesses. I had my share of weaknesses! Yes, I used drugs and alcohol, but those substances are short-lived. They dull the voices and emotional pain for a while, and then it's "back to the real world."

So you want to know my personal experience? I went straight up to the light, and I didn't have a tunnel. My grandmother was there and said to me, "What the hell did you do? You have a family who loves you, fans who love you." But I'm NOT sorry I did it. I'm sure that many of the spirits that you have channeled, during your career, who killed themselves have remorse. But I don't have regrets because I was tired, not scared, just plain tired.

Like you, my work was my life. It's all that I knew. People don't understand how draining it is to channel spirits because it looks effortless, but when you're in your own skin, it's exhausting. You make being a medium look easy, and I made comedy and acting look easy. But the work takes its toll.

If I could say to people that it's not right to take your life, I would. But that action depends on the circumstance and the cause of what's prompting the person to do it. I never believed in Heaven or Hell—that's a religious thing. I do believe in love—that's a healing thing. There is love here, there is light here, there is forgiveness here and there is acceptance here. I am fine and still alive, more alive than I've ever been, but without mental, emotional or physical pain. Later, I might teach souls who arrive what it's like to be an "empath" like I was and like you are. We are misunderstood artists, loners of sorts. I so understand your pain. It's nice to know that I can give you this information and that you understand me as well.

To kill or not to kill, that is the question. Religion says thou shalt not kill. But religion in itself is not an individual entity gripped with pain. I believe religion is for the masses and not for diverse and unique individuals. That's my personal take on it, if you know what I mean. I do not know of a gray area, but I don't beg to differ. There has to be a place where jerks go.

For now I'm still reviewing my life. I almost pity myself! So the act of suicide is not an issue with me. Not yet anyway. The regret I have is hurting my family, causing them pain and that is all.

I did what I wanted to do this last life. There is a prewritten destiny, I believe, for everyone. So far I'm not condemned, I'm not in hell. I'm in a place of peace and light. I like it here. The public needs to know that dying is not cut and dry. They need to know that not every suicide victim goes to hell. Everyone needs to lighten up—laugh more and love more. I wanted to tell you that there are many variables here and not all go through a tunnel, see angels or get their wings. The good part is we all look around age 30. No wrinkles, no baldness, no humpbacks.

So that's all. We do retain our personalities, but not our pain.

For now I'm signing off and happy to contribute.

I salute you!

12

American Indian Proud

What an awesome sight to behold! I'm sitting on a balcony at a renowned resort, overlooking a rock strewn waterfall. Nature is soothing for the soul, and all the guests at the resort seem peaceful and happy. I'm listening to the rhythmic sound of the waterfall on this rather cool July day. There have been times when I have actually seen American Indian spirits from the past, walking this land. Birds, deer, black bear and many other creatures add to the feeling of "going back in time" to a quieter, simpler way of life. Today though, here in the Poconos, an old wise American Indian from many moons ago sits across from me. He is willing to share his story.

My name means "Strong like Bear." I see you are writing a book on the Great Beyond as we called it. Our deceased ancestors we called the "sky people." A spirit will keep its personality and consciousness when we cross to the beyond. Many become one with others in their "soul consciousness" or group, especially if they have had more earthly incarnations together. The more human existences a soul has had, the larger their soul group with ancestors and friends will be. I have retained my integrity and the ways of our people. I do not wish to enter earth again, at least not for a long time.

I want to talk about ancestral lines, which may have confused people in the past. A spirit is a body of light and energy which can incarnate as a male or female. A spirit can also choose a culture, race or a religious background to be born into. My spirit could have incarnated into a white (Caucasian), black (African-American) or yellow

(Asian) baby boy or girl body. Or I could come back as an American Indian in your present time.

You may call me stubborn, but I am "American Indian Proud." I lived in these very mountains and woods in the 1700s and we were a free people. There were tribes like the Ottawa and some others from Canada who migrated to the east. We were a peaceful, spiritual, simple people who revered all of Great Spirit's creations, whether they were bird, animal, fish, rock or tree. My wife "Small Otter" was a dedicated companion, although we did not marry as you do now. We had a ceremony and asked the blessings of our two families and ancestors. We exchanged simple, traditional things, like animal skins, feathers and handmade clothing articles.

In the "Great Beyond," I do not want to leave this way of being, because of loving memories that I have for that lifetime. But when I am ready to rejoin the earth people, I do not wish to be an American Indian again.

We have the ability to see the earth people and what they are doing at so-called viewing stations. I see now the poverty, alcoholism, drug abuse and diabetic conditions that many of the American Indians endure. It is so different now in your time and culture then it was in ours, many moons ago. So for now I will stay in spirit, in this place of the beyond, without abuse, competition or fast-paced living.

I wanted to repeat again that a spirit can re-enter earth and choose a different ancestral line, race or part of the world to be born into. I have not had many lifetimes on earth—only five. Therefore, I like it here and want to study and learn about your earth, but not live in your world. We are never forced to learn or be born or to choose anything. We have free choice. For now, I just want to remember my last life—the beauty of nature and our simple ways. It takes courage to be born into a situation that is new and different.

More advanced spirits here, who have had many lifetimes on earth and in many different cultures and parts of the world, are known to us as "older souls." These older souls have had more earthly experiences and have learned more soul lessons. You would probably call me a younger soul, as I still retain a stubborn streak and I'm not open to new ways of doing things right now. We have much time here to decide what to do in the future. We do not have day and night or seasons of the year as you do in your world. I do miss the seasons, the elements and nature.

This is what I wanted to give you, as a "gift" for your book. This was my decision. I would like earth people to know that they can be forced on earth to do things against their will, but in our Great Beyond, there is no forcing—only freedom and individual decisions.

Strong Like Bear

13

Persecution to Forgiveness

As I have stated previously, I believe in the power of protective prayer. Each morning I visualize the white light of God surrounding me and pray that only souls from Heaven communicate for the highest good of all, providing truth.

I was taken back one day when after my prayers I saw, sitting before me, what looked like a lady who lived a few centuries ago. She projected as a plain lady, wearing a long dress with a cape and bonnet. The emphasis of her story was about forgiveness rather than persecution. I was eager to include it in this book.

Persecution to Forgiveness

My name is Mary, and I want to tell you my story. There was a time in history when people were very superstitious. I loved nature, herbs and plants and kept a large garden. People would visit me to receive information on using herbs to heal themselves and to invigorate others. I lived alone outside of town and never wanted to marry or have children. Stray cats were attracted to my garden, because there was a plant similar to catnip that they loved to chew. Cats were my main companions, and I always had at least seven or eight around. In those days people didn't believe in keeping cats inside or even letting them enter past the threshold of the front door. I thought these superstitions were nonsense, and I always had at least three inside to keep me company. Staying to myself, I enjoyed sewing, preserving fruits and putting herbal remedies together for the townspeople.

One day a couple of men knocked on my door and said they were taking me to town to stand trial. There was panic in the town about so-called witches that were defined by several criteria—living alone, working with unconventional medicinal plants, harboring cats and not attending church every Sunday! It seems the whole town was hypnotized with this nonsense.

At first I thought these men were joking, but I grabbed my shawl and bonnet and off we went. They took me straight to a courtroom of sorts with a lot of men and women sitting in rows. There must've been 200 to 300 people sitting on benches that rose up diagonally towards the ceiling. Two judges sat behind a huge table while a few women were hysterically crying. The crowd in the room shouted, "Hang them! Hang them!"

Our hands were tightly tied behind our backs with rope. Each one of us, on that particular day, had to go and stand before the judges who I didn't know. It seemed the men in the courtroom were the most agitated about the whole situation. Women, wearing black dresses and white capes, were rather silent, even as the crowd grew louder.

So there I was in a nightmare, defending myself for nothing I had done wrong. Church records were exposed, and they counted how many times I attended the town church. I believed in God and prayed every day at my home, but I was a loner of sorts. Being in large groups of people frustrated me. I wasn't afraid of large groups; I just would rather be by myself with my own thoughts.

They called me a witch—plain and simple! Rather than try to defend myself, I stood in shock and disbelief. On the first day, this trial took several hours. We weren't allowed to leave the courtroom even if we had to relieve ourselves. I knew only two of the other women that day. One had come to me for herbal remedies, and the other was her sister. Both women lived alone together, and I thought they were sweet and kind—only to be told that they too were evil witches!

After many hours of interrogation, the other women and I were taken to a makeshift holding area. We were exhausted from questions like, "What did we do at night, why do we keep familiars provided by Satan (the cats), why didn't we attend church every Sunday and why were we against the town doctors by pulling people away from conventional medicine to natural cures?"

All of this happened so quickly, but it was unwarranted. Some of the families who came to my small farm to buy herbal remedies would not speak up on my behalf because of fear. Anyone who had been associated with us might also be considered witches.

The judges voted on our sentence; we were to be hanged! The next morning, at dawn, we heard hammering of wood, and they took us to be hanged. Now there was a huge crowd, all of the townspeople it seemed. There were two posts with a horizontal beam. The two sisters were crying and loudly pleading, but for some reason I remained calm.

Then I found out the very worst thing that had happened! They went to my land and tried to catch all of my cats. The men caught four of them—the three inside my cabin and one of my favorites from the field. That is when I spoke up, "Please don't kill my cats!" The crowd laughed and before I knew it my cats were all put into a big bag, tied with a rope at the top. My cats were to be drowned!

Next we were taken to the gallows, but right before they hung me my soul was out of my body and I was looking down from an aerial view. My soul left my body even before I died! My spirit rose higher and higher until the crowd in the town grew smaller and disappeared. I no longer heard wailing, my cats crying or the other frenzied women. I floated along a bright light filled channel. When I got to the end of that beam of light, there were beings of love waiting for me. Some I recognized as deceased family members, my parents in particular, and some I never met. They said, "Mary, we are sorry for your death on earth, but you now have peace."

I did not see the souls of the other women that died with me that morning. But after a while in this place of light, I went through a review. I did not want to relive my execution, but I had to. In that review I felt the fear of the crowd that shouted hysterically. They feared for their own lives! I was then asked by angelic looking beings if I could forgive those who persecuted me. I thought about the accusations, the trial and my execution. I just couldn't understand these new rules of the town, and why we were called evil. The kind angelic beings explained that it was nothing I did wrong, that the persecution of me and the others was a misconceived notion that stemmed from fear. They told me that fear begets fear, and love begets love.

"Was I ready to forgive?" the light beings asked me once again. The confusion about what happened left me, and again I felt the horrific fear of the town's people (in a mass consciousness way). I *could* forgive them, and I did. I did not have to forgive individuals; I had to forgive the "mass" of people and the concept of their fear based actions. Some people, and even souls, have held onto a persecution feeling, but I knew in my heart I had to let it go.

Everyone dies in a different way, sooner or later. You might say I was at the wrong place at the wrong time, but I feel that my demise was meant to be. In this place of light I want to help souls and counsel them about forgiveness, for this action is important to help them spiritually move on. It can be very difficult to forgive, release anger and love others. It may be that *forgiveness* is one of the hardest lessons to learn, but I feel it should be done, either while on earth or in Heaven.

In God's grace,
Mary

14

Spirit Rehabilitation

When I was 14, my biological father passed away from a brain tumor. It was difficult growing up without a father, as I dearly loved him. There was another couple, Alma and Ted that my parents were very close to and socialized with. After my father passed away, my mother went to Europe with her best friend, Alma. Upon returning, Alma had a massive, fatal heart attack. A few months later Ted, now a widower, asked my mother out, and they eventually got married.

My new stepfather, Ted, was well educated, a world traveler and served as a Lieutenant Colonel in the Army. He collected many valuables, especially books. When Ted crossed over, he left behind almost 1,000,000 books, antiques and quite a collection of other objects. The artifacts were housed in a church that Ted had purchased. Dispersing of all his belongings was an exhausting process that included more than 15 public auctions.

He always liked me and supported my artwork. When his spirit spontaneously stopped by to say hello, I was in my office between counseling sessions. What surprised me was Ted's candid information about the collection of his things. He now understood that he was a hoarder, sharing the account of his rehabilitation in Heaven!

Hoarding

Michele, you know that I was a hoarder, collecting more than a million books and lots of antiques and then buying a church to house them. Even though you are a good artist, Michele, your ability to communicate with the spirit world is much needed now, and you have the determination to be a good medium.

In this higher place, I connect with your mother on occasion. I hold you most dear, because I always thought well of you and respected your talents. I may not have been so kind to my own children, but you seemed special. I wasn't perfect, but I tried in my own way to do what was right.

I need to tell you about the soul place that you're writing about. First, as an "energy being" we can walk through walls and walk-through each other. We can fly or think of a part of the world that we want to see, and we are there! Those reading your book may question all of this information, but when you think of energy, you think of currents. Our souls are comprised of energy currents, and energy can never be destroyed. Eventually the physical world loses its grip upon us. *Stuff* is not what is important. You can't take the stuff with you, as everyone knows.

Over here I'm still very interested in books, not reading them, but viewing authors that are now writing on earth. I know other souls have mentioned viewing stations, but I myself like to go to an old movie theater of sorts. The kind of theaters they had years ago when the black-and-white silent movies were popular starring Charlie Chaplin, and the slapstick talkies of Laurel and Hardy. In those days these were theaters with red velvet seats and a thick velvet curtain in front of the screen. If I want to view any authors, metaphysical or not, I can view them when the curtain is drawn back. Other energy beings who are interested in viewing people on earth can join me. History is fascinating to me, and if you remember, I was a Lieutenant Colonel in the Army. So historical authors, who are now writing about past wars or military subjects, interest me.

I was of the Catholic faith while on earth, so I expected to immediately see some of the saints when I crossed over.

At the end in the hospital I was confused. My bladder cancer took hold of me, and I was also on strong pain medication. So needless to say, I was quite surprised after I passed away to first see my little daughter, Paula, waiting for me. She passed from leukemia at age four and wanted to look that age so I would recognize her. I also saw my first wife, my parents and some other relatives. In the beginning they looked like silhouettes with misty light around them. But as I moved forward towards them, the light got much brighter and I could see them all. A couple of beings floated up to me and embraced me. I knew then that people are more important than things. Your readers need to know that hoarding is a form of sickness.

You know that I drank alcohol, and that numbed the pain of my life. Collecting and hoarding gave me a sense of control over things. I could not prevent my little child from dying, or my dysfunctional family situation from childhood into adulthood, but I could control my things. Those objects weren't leaving me or talking back! People sometimes hoard animals like cats or dogs for this reason. You'll find more hoarding of cats in your society now, because they are quiet (not like barking dogs), and they don't need to go outside.

So after my heartfelt reunion, spirit counselors asked if I thought that I needed rehabilitation. Even though the "energy current" leaves the body, there still can be a slight residue of emotional dysfunction. Yes, we do keep our mind, personality, memory bank and consciousness intact, as you share in your seminars. The concept of rehabilitation will be new and probably controversial for your readers, but that's okay. Each soul who has conversed with you has shared what they want to share. So if nothing else, this book is "food for thought."

Everything is so organized on earth, whether it's different religions, the military or the political arena. The masses, most of the time, do not think outside the box, and some don't think at all (Ted laughs). Counselors here are spirits who have been in the same emotional position that we have been while on earth. The psychologists that a human being goes to in the physical world have not experienced everything that their clients are dealing with. They go to school, get a degree and apply what they have learned to help others. There is an old saying, "You can't really understand another person's experience until you have walked a mile in their shoes."

Now think how great it is to be counseled here by a few spirits who emotionally understand you! I was really helped when I saw replays of my life. My review wasn't fast; it seemed to take a long time. I saw how I cheated on a test in college, how I used the military to be in control and how I treated my first wife and children. I did mellow as I got older, so when I met your mother, I was much more flexible and kind.

The other thing that was very clear in my review was how I used stuff to placate myself, and again to help me feel in control. Objects that I collected (whether books, postcards, glassware or Asian antiques) were a part of my emotional community. The spirit counselors who had been hoarders and lived a similar life really understood me, and I in turn understood myself. When you live in a dark trench, you are unaware of the truth or the light, as you call it.

I'm glad you took the time to listen and write all of this down. In regards to hoarding, people that read this will understand that there is hope for those on earth, but there can be healing in this "higher realm" as well. Eventually, all in this realm will be healed and cleansed. There is so much to do here spiritually, but I wanted to share that we still can pursue study, make choices and be with other energy currents of like mind.

I bid you adieu and I love you,

Ted

My best friend in early childhood was a little boy named Ricky. We were both born in 1951, and he lived across the street with his younger brother in a big white stucco house. I remember my mother saying that Ricky's dad was sick and had to go to the hospital every few weeks for dialysis. I also remember his mother had a foreign accent and was very shy. Ricky and I went to kindergarten, elementary school and high school together. When we were in elementary school, his father died of kidney failure. We reconnected at a high school reunion many years later and were able to catch up on all of our years apart. He shared that his mother never remarried and did not like to go out. She ended up living with Ricky's younger brother. Then a few years later his mother passed away.

After the high school reunion, I lost track of Ricky, but he "friended" me one day on a social media site in 2009. One evening in January 2015, I had the unexplained urge to send a message to Ricky, wishing him a "Happy New Year." Little did I know that his deceased mother would communicate with me the very next day!

I was preparing lunch in the kitchen when I first felt his mother's overwhelming presence. Then I heard her soft voice say, "Hello Michele, this is Mrs. B." Once again I quickly found a pen and paper and sat down at the kitchen table to write down her experiences.

Depression

I hope you remember me; I'm your neighbor that lived across the street when you were little. You went to school with my son, Ricky. Thank you for getting in touch with him last night. I prompted that. I'm proud of him, but my other son has some problems. We can help our children from this side by trying to keep them positive and on track, but first we need to get ourselves on track. My husband was a brilliant engineer. If you remember, he died, and I was a widow when you and my son were growing up. I never remarried and was very depressed. I really should have been on medication, but in the 1950s people didn't share things like that with their doctors.

They were scared (like I was) that the doctors wouldn't believe them, or they would put them away in an institution. They did lobotomies then, and everyone was afraid of them.

I too was afraid of everything—being alone, not having enough money, and even being a burden on family and friends. Most of my family was still overseas in Europe, which made my fear worse. I want to share what it was like for me to cross over, because I held onto this fear for most of my life. I learned later that I was a self-induced manic depressive but did not want to be on medication.

My children and grandchildren were there for me at the end of my life. I took my last breath and after leaving my body, I saw my beloved husband. Les had died from kidney failure and had been on dialysis for quite awhile. Well Les looked good in the spirit world and very happy. He took my hand and said, "Come with me."

We entered a very large room that looked like a ballroom where I saw my deceased family from the old country. They projected both young and old, and exactly as I remembered them. We greeted one another, and I felt like I was truly home. At this point I wasn't confused, shy or timid but still a little scared.

After the reunion my guardian angel came for me and told me we had some work to do! I didn't know that you still worked in Heaven. The angel led me to another big room, and there sat some beings that I didn't recognize. They told me that they were spiritual counselors of light, and wanted to telepathically talk to me. I sat down and listened.

They asked me why I still felt afraid. I then realized that for most of my life my decisions were fear based. Fear is a very negative emotion. I was lonely and it was hard for me to make friends when I came to America. I guess you would call this experience a "review" of my life. It was on a big movie screen. I saw all of the decisions I made from the time I was little until the time I died. I wasn't born with fear in the old country, but I was a little shy, it seemed. As a child I wanted to please everyone, and so I gave in and let other people make decisions for me and my life. I understood that I was not crazy, that my depression was not hereditary but self-induced. We were not told in those days about positive thinking, how to honor yourself or how to make love-based decisions as you now call them.

After I witnessed myself and my actions in my last life, I was asked a question: "What could I have done differently to love myself?" It seemed like a long process, not a quick one. Once I realized that my fear was self-induced, I could release it. I guess some people who die leave behind all of their negative emotions, but I carried a residue of fear over with me. I was in God's light, but still felt a little held back.

The spirit counselors had me repeat, "I love myself, I love myself." I remembered that we're all equal and worthy. After I was able to acknowledge that, I had a healing in Heaven! My healing didn't happen my last lifetime on earth, but in Heaven.

I understood that these counselors of light were also healers of other newly arrived spirits. I know that sounds funny to say, but it's true. Those reading this, who are depressed, I hope you realize that if your condition is not hereditary, it is probably self-induced through your thoughts.

If I could have remembered this information and used it for my highest good on earth, I would have had a happier life. I know I surprised you, Michele, by coming by to chat, but this information is to let people know that they are loved. And also it's okay to love and honor yourself. Even though some of the physical death, transition and life review experiences in your book on Heaven will be somewhat similar, they're not all exactly the same. Before I could fully relax I needed to release my worst enemy—*fear!*

Mrs. B

There was a group of us who regularly got together to share our healing gifts and spiritual experiences. At one of these get-togethers I met Donna, a nurse, massage therapist and Reiki Master. She was considered a brilliant healer.

One time I twisted my right leg and a large lump developed behind my knee. At the next get together, she called me into a private room and laid her hands on the back of my right knee. I felt intense heat emanating from her hands, going into my leg. To my surprise, the next morning the lump was completely dissolved!

She shared some childhood issues with me, and I was shocked to hear that her own father had sexually abused her from age four until she was 12. It was a struggle for her to forgive and move on, but Donna was an emotional survivor. I feel her desire to heal others was her driving force, because of her own abuse. She told me that she felt unconditional love from her pets and loved all animals. When my husband and I traveled, she was our official pet sitter.

In time our paths drifted apart and we lost contact with each other. Years later, I received an envelope in the mail that contained Donna's obituary. She had passed away of uterine cancer. I sent some prayers up for her, that she would be at peace and happy in the light.

My husband and I were vacationing in Jamaica when I contracted a bad case of prickly heat, confining me to our room. We loved the small resort on the beach, and every time we vacationed there I'd feed the numerous stray cats. I was resting when I distinctly heard Donna's voice. It shocked me because I hadn't thought of her in a very long while. I surmised that my love of the cats at the resort and my alone time brought the energy of her soul through.

I urgently took the hotel's notepad and started to write. Donna talked about her childhood abuse, her love of animals and (interestingly enough) her involvement with rehabilitating souls on the other side:

Abuse

Guess you didn't think you'd hear from me on your vacation, but it's Donna! Well I'm up here, and here is a wonderful place. I now work with hurting human souls, along with the welfare of the animal consciousness. The light bodies that I work with were sexually abused while in their physical bodies. Even though their physical body is no longer present here, some still have slight emotional scars. The scars I'm referring to are primarily from the ones who were sexually abused as children. A lot of this happens on earth, more than you will ever know!

As I have shared with you before, I was abused at a young age by my dad, which messed me up for a long time. Nursing and Reiki are healing modalities, and I first wanted to heal myself from my own torment, then help others. Souls are pure beings from God, but as you know we retain our personalities. So on this side I openly share my story with others who have been in the same predicaments. It seems to help them at our spiritual gathering, which is like a "therapy group."

Acknowledging forgiveness is so important during these sessions that I lead. On occasion spirits may "get stuck" in a way of thinking, even after their life review. Forgiving someone who you loved and *trusted* as a child, but who hurt you, is a very difficult thing to do. We arrive at the realization that these abuses come from emotionally hurting human beings who in turn hurt us. We cannot see their life reviews, but we can learn to understand these individuals. The greatest progress that a soul can make to move on spiritually is to let go and forgive.

My father was an alcoholic, and many times didn't realize or care how his sexual molestation would affect me. Now I'm talking from about four years old to 12, and that's a long time. I have met up with my father's soul here, and I've told him that I forgive him.

Because I myself was a hurting person on earth, I also wanted to help animals for they were my true friends. My pets showed me unconditional love when no one else could. I believe my mother knew about the abuse but turned a blind eye as sometimes mothers do when they are scared. So I don't fault her. I told her when I was 12, and she believed me then. After that she left my dad, who remained a drunk.

I got my period when I was 12, and my dad didn't like that. So when the torture of molestation stopped, I felt free to tell my mom. Honestly, I don't think she would have left him anyway until she had some money saved.

As you know I was gay. Sometimes sexual abuse as a child will create lesbians and sometimes not. In my "soul review," I learned that I had been a man in several past earthly incarnations and had a few lifetimes as American Indian males.

I also want you to know that I am a volunteer to rehab animal spirits from the canine and feline consciousness. When animals have been abused through neglect, ignorance or for financial gain (like pit bull fighting), it lowers the overall frequency of that consciousness. Sometimes people can be so greedy at the expense of the poor animals. When cats or dogs die they go back into their own feline or canine consciousness. When I refer to consciousness, I mean an energy frequency. Animals do not possess human souls. And when someone has truly loved their pet, it raises the whole animal consciousness level. On the other hand, when a person abuses or tortures an animal it lowers the animal consciousness through fear. Love heals and uplifts; fear destroys and negates.

Dogs (canine), cats (feline), horses (equine) and so on are separate groups of energy, but they can still retain individual memories after they merge back into their own consciousness. People tend to try to "humanize" their pets and some "old soul" pets (animals that have had more earthly incarnations), seem to be more humanized. Humane treatment of all species is crucial. Our awareness of animals' emotions needs to be understood. I see that you are trying to help with the cat population on earth the best way you can, and it does make a difference, helping them one by one. Showing charity to homeless cats or dogs is advantageous for both the human and the animal. No love is ever wasted.

You know that I died of uterine cancer, and that is an area where I psychologically held my pain from the abuse. I have really moved on in this world of light, and I enjoy what I do here. Some spirits just want to enjoy Heaven and not do much for a while, and that's okay, as there is no time in this dimension. But since I have been over here for quite a while, I grew tired of "playing" and wanted to make a difference in Heaven, as I tried to do on earth.

I'm signing off now. Glad to talk to you. Be happy on earth while you can and take care of yourself.

Your friend,
Donna

15

Astral Travel

When I started this book I had so many questions about "life after life." What was it like to let go of the physical body? What is Heaven really like? Where do souls go who commit heinous crimes? For the answers I would never try and "pull" a soul down to the earth plane to communicate, nor would I want to. All have free choice and free will.

As previously stated, prayer and meditation was a crucial part of preparation for each session. I would always pray for accurate information to come through for humanities highest good.

One morning, after my spiritual preparation, I had a surprise. A light body appeared wearing a robe and sandals with a docile demeanor. He called himself a "spokesman" and told me his name was Mark. He simply wanted to share information about the concept of astral travel and relayed this dialogue:

Have you ever had dreams of loved ones who have crossed over? I'm here to discuss the fact that the light body doesn't leave the physical body just upon death. The light body of a person can leave during sleep time and meet us here in the fourth dimension.

My name is Mark. I come as a spokesman to tell you that there is webbing between souls still in physical bodies on earth and souls free from the attachment of physical bodies in this realm. If you have deeply loved someone on earth and they pass away, there are still heart strings attached. The bond of love can never be broken, thus creating this webbing. Your soul can leave during sleep and astral travel through your connecting portal to meet with us.

As was discussed in another dissertation, the light body enters the baby body with the first breath; it enters through the top of the baby's head and attaches itself at the solar plexus region. The navel is where the soul's umbilical cord, also called the "silver cord," is attached. This cord can stretch, allowing the light body to leave the physical body at will, which is called an OBE or "out of body experience." Those who consciously know how to leave can do so at any time of the day or night and return safely to their physical bodies.

There are souls who want to travel up to the astral world to be mentored or to work out their earthly problems. Souls residing here can go down toward earth and souls inhabiting an earthly body can rise up to meet them via astral travel. When I am referring to traveling "up and down," I mean the souls in the higher and lower frequencies can meet somewhere in the middle.

A mother, for example, who is having problems with her son's drug abuse, can travel at night to this higher frequency. Her soul can converse with others from her soul group who may show her how to cope with her son's substance abuse. The mother may also meet up with souls who were clinical psychologists, doctors or rehab counselors when they lived on earth. She may then suddenly awaken with peace and have a hopeful outlook on her son's drug addiction prognosis, or she may intuitively know how to help him.

At times people awaken with amazing ideas for musical compositions, creative writing styles or themes for developing a series of paintings. These occurrences come from the mentorship they receive from us, here in the higher dimension. I would advise that if someone needs help or an answer to a pressing question, that they write the request on a piece of paper and put it in their pillowcase before sleep. I would also advise for them to say an affirmation of protection before going to sleep.

If a person's light body has been astral traveling, he or she may have dreams of flying, falling, running or going underwater before awakening. This indicates that their light body is returning to their physical body. I wanted to share the fact that we can not only communicate through dreams, electrical occurrences and other ways from the fourth dimension, but can actually help those on earth, either at night in the astral world or with an OBE during the day.

16

Ascended Masters

Today, when I look over at the spirit chair, I am startled to see an elegant young woman whom I do not know, at least in this present lifetime. She has dark, thick hair parted in the middle and worn up, deep blue eyes and a long graceful neck. Her gown is draped over her body in flowing white silk. She projects wearing a single baroque pearl necklace and gold bangle bracelets travel up her left arm. This delicate beauty also wears sandals and appears peaceful and serene. I ask what her name is and why she came to converse. Souls work with me telepathically by sending pictures and feelings, so there is no need for them to move their lips. The lady sits very still, reminding me of an exquisitely carved, pristine marble statue. Then she speaks:

My name is Aspasia, and my last lifetime was in ancient Greece. I am not a spirit guide of yours, but I come with important information. I teach about love, beauty and compassion in this dimension and I work with some of the ascended masters—those who have no need to reincarnate, but rather stay here to enlighten human souls. I want to first say that indeed there is a Higher Power which some call God—the Creator. God is pure unconditional love and is encapsulated in everything in nature—in the elements of earth, air, fire and water, in every tree, mountain and animal. That divine love is in the DNA of the human cellular structure. I want to address the advanced realm of the ascended ones.

Ascended Masters

There are numerous ascended masters to study with in this realm and to invoke for help while inhabiting earth. They are spiritually enlightened beings, who in past incarnations were ordinary humans with extraordinary transformations! A human being who has regained full union with the mighty "I Am Presence" is an ascended one. Ascended masters have raised their energetic vibration and their consciousness to a higher frequency of light. They have transcended all human limitations and have manifested their mastery over all that is human. Ascended ones are the pure embodiment of light, love and the purity of virtues. I would like to mention a few.

One such master is St. Germain, who transmutes energy to a higher vibration by carrying a violet flame. He helps to assist light workers when they do healing work on earth.

An individual may be drawn to the energy of St. Francis of Assisi, the patron saint of animals. St. Francis was a Franciscan monk who had the ability to communicate with all animals and birds, bringing peace and healing to them. Remember that sometimes an *animal* can also be the *teacher* of unconditional love.

The Master Jesus embodies the Christ Consciousness and is considered to be the Son of God. His essence has to do with manifesting miracles, dissolving fear and restoring wellness to mind, body and spirit.

Buddha in the East taught that the way to enlightenment is to go within oneself through meditation. This practice provides focus, calmness, concentration and awareness.

Confucius, who was born in 551 BC, is considered an ascended master. He compiled many writings about the virtues and how to strive for the light in every thought, word and deed.

There is a contemporary master with us named Padre Pio, who was born in 1887 in Italy. He became a priest, bore the wounds of Christ for 50 years and had the gift of prophecy. Padre Pio was known for his bi-location (the ability to be in a couple different places simultaneously). This master could also "read souls" and create miraculous cures.

These are the male ascended masters that I personally work with. But there are many female ascended ones as well like Blessed Mother Mary, Quan Yin and Mary Magdalene.

So you see, ascended ones that you feel close to or want to invoke can be male or female. The earth plane has always been predominantly male oriented with patriarchal societies. The female ascended ones are powerful in the way of instilling gentle love and empathy. They truly bring this concept to earth.

Blessed Mother Mary is also called "Mother of the World," and she especially protects women and children. As the "Queen of the Angels," she personifies divine feminine qualities, nurturing energy and intercedes in healing.

There has been controversy as to Mary Magdalene's role with Jesus. She walked beside the Christ as an emissary of truth. Some feel she was His bride, but Mary Magdalene was indeed a counterpart of Christ in female form. In biblical times she was deemed a prostitute but was a learned scholar, healer and messenger of light.

Quan Yin is known as the Asian "Mother Mary of the East." Her essence is pure mercy and tenderness.

The energy of the ascended masters resides in a very high frequency. This is a place of golden light which houses a transparent crystal city, known as the "City of God." The masters teach here, or they can be invoked to come down to earth and work with you.

It was my pleasure to share this information,

Aspasia

17

Animal Consciousness

I was fortunate to have an inspiring client named Cynthia in the early 1990s who became a dear friend. She had a prestigious job with the state, but her true job was the love and caretaking of animals. She developed a nonprofit organization to spay, neuter and house homeless animals. When Cynthia passed away, she left all of her money to benefit her foundation. She never married or had children, so her pets were her family.

At a relatively young age, she developed a brain tumor, and I was thankful that I was able to visit her at her home just before she died. One night, a few months after she passed away, I had a vision of her. Cynthia was wearing a purple robe with a hood. She telepathically sent to me that she was with her beloved pets, but also added, "I'm not sure I like what they did to my house!"

Not knowing what the last part of the message meant about her house, I called another one of her friends to find out. Yes, it was confirmed that her house sold almost immediately after she passed away, and the new owners totally revamped and restructured it. She was not a materialistic person, but the message she gave me about her home was a confirmation that the spirit world can still see what happens here on earth.

Then one sunny morning in June, I was anxious to see what spirit was going to communicate with me for this book. I was so delighted that it was my friend Cynthia, who appeared in a beautiful shade of fuchsia:

Hello, it's good to telepathically communicate with you. I loved my life, the people who surrounded me and especially my pets. Although the nonprofit organization that I initially founded geared to homeless cats, I'm glad to see that the organization now helps dogs as well. I loved all animals, and the work of my foundation pleases me. Thank you for coming over to visit me before I died, for praying with me and for your "laying on of hands." All was appreciated.

There is so much to do in Heaven, but today I want to talk about the animal kingdom. I understand that there are people who love their pets more than they do other people. I was probably one of them while living on earth.

In this dimension, there is an animal consciousness for each species that human souls can interact with. If souls so choose, they can become a caretaker, not only for their own pets, but also their favorite groups of animals, like tigers (feline) or wolves (canine) for example. Here animals do not have individual human souls as we do, but gather with the consciousness of their own species.

You are correct when you state in your other book, *Messages from Beyond*, that animals have a "mass consciousness of energy" like feline, canine or equine among others. Personally, I have chosen to work with the feline consciousness along with doing other forms of spiritual work.

You can incarnate with other human souls who remain in your soul group, but also animals from their own consciousness can contract to be with you from lifetime to lifetime as well. I fell in love with felines in two of my Egyptian lifetimes. The smaller wildcats were introduced into Egypt from Persia, but the Egyptians also revered larger cats like leopards and cheetahs. Many of the big cats were raised from kittens and guarded queens' and court servants' quarters. Additionally the larger cats were sometimes chained around the bathhouses of the servant women to protect them from intruders.

Certain spirits here just enjoy being in the *energy* of the animal consciousnesses. Spirits can volunteer to "pet sit" relatives' deceased pets until their owners join them in Heaven. Other souls just want to be near the feline or canine consciousness, because they loved cats or dogs in general.

There is no designated area where these animals reside, as the energy of the animal consciousness overlaps our human soul energy. But we as souls can *create* environments with our thought forms and therefore some souls (I have observed) will create an estate with horses, dogs and cats. When they create this type of environment, the species of animals that they desire will pull out of their own "energy consciousness." In other words, some of these animals are not from the person's own soul group, nor did the animals have any physical contact with them while on earth.

I am not obsessed with the energy of animals as a number of souls in Heaven are, but I like to occasionally visit my pets. There is an enchanting emerald green hill that I have created with my thought forms. I relax on top of this lush hill and all of my beloved pets from past incarnations visit me. They are happy and visually look like kittens or puppies. My pets romp and play, making my heart laugh and my soul sing. There is nothing like the sweetness of seeing these innocent creatures having fun, and it brings me such joy!

Not only does my soul pop down to see how my animal foundation is doing, but in addition I try to intervene and play a role in trap, neuter, return (TNR) for feral cat colonies on earth. My mission is to induce positive thoughts, not only for my own volunteers, but also for other animal organizations. When I say my soul "plays a role" I mean I can influence (but never force) the minds of physical beings on earth to become more involved with helping stray animals. I like to encourage those in the physical world to lend their energy, time and money to help homeless animals find good homes.

Even though I desperately didn't want to leave the earth, the timeline that I soul contracted was up. But now all of my blessed pets are with me and I feel complete.

I would like to add that not all of my intentions go to the animal kingdom. I'm also involved with learning about compassion from the Ascended Masters.

I wish you well, Michele, with this book and all of your endeavors. It was an honor to talk to you today. I'm sending love and blessings,

Cynthia

For the last eight years my husband Jon and I have had the opportunity to lecture and do consultations at an exclusive spa resort in the Pocono Mountains in Pennsylvania. One afternoon I had some free time there and went out on a balcony to view the waterfall and imbibe the clean, fresh smell of evergreens. I sat down, enjoying the warmth of the sun. While relaxing, I glanced over at the empty chair beside me, and to my surprise, a female spirit was sitting next to me. She appeared with short blonde hair, blue eyes and was wearing a light blue denim shirt with khaki work pants. I did not recognize her because we had never met while she lived on earth. She telepathically told me her name was Dee and proceeded to tell a story about her farm life in the 1900s, placing much emphasis on the animals she loved. The following is her account:

My name is Dolores, but you can call me Dee. I've come to talk to you about the animals I cared for. I grew up on a working farm in Ohio in the early 1900s. My life was simple then. We had cows, goats, horses, dogs, cats and chickens. From an early age I loved the animals, and since we were a working farm, some cows were slaughtered for meat. We also had cow and goat milk that we made into cream and cheese. Our chickens provided eggs of course, and some of them were killed for their meat. I fell in love with every animal on the farm, giving each of them individual names—including each chicken!

My younger brother was strong-willed, and he didn't want to do farm chores or take care of the animals. He was assigned to feeding them, while I was assigned to milking the cows and goats. I loved to ride our two horses and often felt they could read my mind. Sometimes when I was riding my chestnut mare, Lucy, she would automatically stop as if she knew there was trouble ahead. Lucy instinctively would stop even before a snake would cross her path. Thankfully my beloved horse lived a long life. I personally never married, staying with my parents and caretaking them to the end of their lives. We also had numerous dogs over the years, and some acted almost human. I could tell what they were thinking at times; at least I thought I could. There were many barn cats, for we didn't get them "fixed" as you do today when you spay female pets and neuter males. At one point we had up to 20 barn cats, all of them good mousers. My mother didn't believe in feeding the cats extra. "They could fend for themselves," she'd say. But I would sneak them meat or milk whenever I could.

The mother animals were always so protective over their young. One spring a mama cat gave birth to six kittens in the corner of the barn. The kittens were about two weeks old when we smelled smoke one morning about 4 a.m. We never found out how the fire got started, but it was a very bad fire. Pa opened the barn doors, and flames emerged. He got the two horses out just in time, and some of the cats still in the barn flew out the door in a panic. In the far corner, through the smoke and flames, I saw the mama cat trying to save her kittens. She was pushing them away while they were trying to nurse. I wasn't sure if their eyes were open by then, but she courageously picked up one at a time in her mouth and carried them to the edge of the barn door. The straw was stoking the fire, but mama cat didn't quit. She kept going back, saving one kitten at a time. As she brought them to the barn door opening, I'd grab them from her and quickly lay them on the ground. There was one kitten left to save as five had been retrieved. But mama never returned with her sixth kitten that morning. We later found her in the ashes, burned to death and overcome with smoke inhalation along with her last kitten. I know this was probably just instinct, as my own mother said, but I saw more than that. I saw an animal with bravery and determination, fiercely protecting her offspring—the babies she so loved. That made a great impression on me. I then realized that I loved animals more than I did people, and that animals would become my life.

After my parents passed away, I rode to town every week to study with the local farm veterinarian. He showed me how to care for our animals that were now my pets. I had to sell some cows, and I was left with one good horse after my favorite horse, Lucy, died. Finally I lived out my days with two retriever dogs and several cats, which by then I let into the farmhouse. What wonderful companions they were!

I caught pneumonia one winter and made transition to this place we call Heaven. The very first friends I saw after floating through my portal were my pets. They talked to me, mind to mind, the way I'm communicating with you now! They welcomed me home and thanked me for being their caretaker.

I did the usual things that I think newly arrived spirits do. First I had a family reunion, met my relatives and those from my soul group. Some from my soul group didn't live with me on earth that last lifetime but said they were my spirit helpers. I *remembered* them once I saw them.

After my life's review, I was asked what I wanted to do. Without hesitation I shouted, "Work with animals!" When we love a pet, that love stays with us, and even though there is no space here, an area is created where our pets reside. There may be people on earth who believe that human spirits can inhabit animals. But I have learned that the animal consciousness is different from the human soul consciousness. So my spirit can't come back to earth and be in a dog's or a horse's body. My spirit can only enter a human body again. But there are animals here who you might call "old souls," because they have saved human lives while on earth. They are very intelligent and have had many incarnations.

Our pets can follow us around Heaven if we so wish. Of course we don't have to give them shelter, feed them or slaughter them for meat. But we *can* love them. In Heaven, I have created a huge farm with my thoughts, for this environment is my passion. I have many animal friends here and that's how I like it. I also enlighten other human spirits about the humane treatment of animals, especially if they have abused them. Abuse in any form, whether it pertains to other humans, animals or birds needs to be addressed! There are souls, during their life review, who have remorse for abusing animals because they can fleetingly feel the animal's distress, fear and emotional pain. Harboring this remorse, they can come to a soul like me to learn more about compassion and the animal consciousness.

There are no predators because there is no food chain here, so spirit animals will not attack each other. Fox frolic with chipmunks, cats with mice, dogs with squirrels, hawks with rabbits and so on. It truly is the "Peaceable Kingdom" in the heavenly realm.

I caretake, not just my own companion pets, but animals that make transition to their own consciousness from abusive situations. Animals need to learn to trust and forgive as we humans do. I am pleased that there are so many animal caretakers here in Heaven. Tell your readers that their beloved pets are safe, happy and loved. Tell them that maybe the first faces they will see upon arrival in Heaven will be the faces of their very best friends—their precious pets.

18

The Crystal City

During the time I was writing this book, I was fascinated with receiving stories from my deceased relatives, clients and friends. But every once in awhile, after centering and praying, I was astonished to see a new spirit I didn't recognize. Each one had their own unique memories to share about their past life on earth. This morning a young Asian girl appeared, petite and delicate. She reminded me of a white porcelain doll; her black hair was parted and worn up. Her demeanor was gentle, and she telepathically conveyed her story with a soft voice. I was excited to hear about her experience and her interpretation of the Crystal City!

My name is Chao Xing which means Morning Star. I want to tell you what I experienced when I came here to this world that you call the other side. Though I have had many past lives, my last incarnation on earth was in the 1700s in China. My family was Buddhist and they had a long standing background of the arts and music. My maternal aunt painted water color flowers and birds on long silk panels, along with our Chinese characters of writing. We fortunately were more affluent than most families at that time. My brother played many types of musical instruments and even wrote his own music. His favorite instrument was the bamboo flute.

I loved to work with fabric, and I too painted on silk and different types of cloth. My painted designs were made into clothing. This ancient tradition was handed down in my family from as far back as the first Chinese Emperor who wore them. My hand-painted fabric was made into jackets with Mandarin type collars, skirts and even small round hats. I did not sew, only created colorful, hand painted cloth. My father also painted on porcelain in the blue on white fashion that was popular at the time. Several of his pieces were exported to Europe.

So I lived a beautiful life. We owned a small property, which was unusual during the 1700s in China. Our land was like a small park with a pond and lovely flowers. People would visit to buy our crafts, and we lived an abundant life.

I died after contracting a respiratory virus similar to pneumonia in the winter of 1747. When I left my body, I heard music and the tinkling of tiny bells. Yet they seemed louder than our local Buddhist temple bells. Rather than floating up as others have said, I walked through a large open drum that some would call a tunnel. My drum had golden sides that glistened like a million suns. At the other end, my ancestors were waiting, some generations going back as far as the great emperors in China! After lots of bows and greetings I went to view my book of life. Compared to others in China with the economic situation at that time, I was considered fortunate. I later learned that I soul contracted a peaceful life to bring beauty and gentleness to the world. My relatives, who I incarnated with, also brought joy by means of music and the arts. We were a very close soul group.

The Crystal City

I searched for the "enlightened one" called Buddha and was told by my guides that Buddha resided in a higher frequency as an "ascended master." I learned that a great prophet came to earth to enlighten each culture and bring truth to the masses. This "truth" was called "the golden rule," which means to love and honor all, as well as yourself. "Where is this place where the ascended masters reside?" I asked. Then one of my spiritual helpers came to escort me, because I had never experienced this higher frequency before. The ascended ones can come down and appear to us if need be, but I learned that to greet them you must ascend to their higher frequency.

There appeared to be a huge city sparkling in the sun, translucent and luminescent. Each crystal building in the city housed an ascended one. The Christ Consciousness was housed in a great structure with a pointed spire, as a cathedral would have. Muhammad resided in a crystal mosque with a dome. And finally I found the Buddha Consciousness. Buddha sat in a crystal temple resembling the ones which are made of wood in old China. I entered this place that was floating in space. The temple was like liquid light, golden in color, and it made me feel warm like melted honey when I entered it. This, to me, was pure love, and it permeated my being.

My spirit helper waited outside the structure as my soul knelt before the Enlightened One. There were rays of light coming from Buddha, emanating and permeating my entire essence. I heard each profound word that he sent to me by telepathic communication. He shared the whole concept of his work and told me that love is truth, and both love and truth lie within the heart of each human being. If we are unbalanced, we forget our perfectness while living on earth and can become negative and fearful. Buddha suggested that I be open to the teachings of the other ascended prophets as well. He said that the prophets taught similar concepts, and that their messages were also about truth and love. He reaffirmed that I should be open to hearing all of them. Buddha concluded by saying that I was a pure being of love, and with that last thought my study with him was done for now.

I learned that we carry our religious belief systems with us, and create what we believe when we arrive in this dimension. So if Christians, for example, want to see Jesus in Heaven, a part of the Christ Consciousness will take that form and appear to them, for that is their belief.

But to continue to study with any of these ascended masters, we must rise to their frequency and visit the Crystal City.

I have gained much insight from the ascended ones, but I have moved on now and I'm delighted to teach souls who want to study with me about painting techniques. With my mind I have chosen to create my own private pond with a footbridge, songbirds and an occasional pair of swans. Here my students gather and imbibe what I have to teach. Many souls study all forms of art and music here, in preparation for their next earthly lifetime.

I am happy to give this information to you, for this place is one of light and grace. I thank you for letting me share my journey.

Chao Xing

19

Choosing Disabilities

My name was James, and I knew Michele in the 1980s. She was an artist then and was showcasing her work at a prestigious arts festival in the east. The annual art show was a well publicized and huge event. Even though I was confined to a wheelchair, I was excited to attend the festival each year. I was drawn into her booth to see her artwork and was instantly touched by the "heart light" I felt there; she painted from her heart. We became fast friends and would talk long hours on the phone. Michele made me laugh, and I felt a kinship with her. I wish to tell my story as a direct narrative. Hopefully my narrative will ensure that there will be no form of re-interpretation. Later I commissioned her to create a couple of amazing paintings for me.

My father was a renowned doctor, and I was his only child. My parents were very frustrated with my health condition because I was born with pulmonary problems. I was also paralyzed from my lower chest region down to my feet. Although I had use of my left hand, my right hand was deformed.

Being restricted in a wheelchair did not stop me from achieving my goals or being independent. I lived in the heart of a bustling city and dealt with the corporate world daily. I did not let my condition get me down, although many days it was annoying.

A few years ago my lungs filled with fluid, making breathing difficult and I finally made transition to the "other side." This place is not really the other side as much as it is a different frequency. Everyone knows that there are TV and radio wavelengths, but you need a conduit to see and hear these frequencies. Michele is a conduit to our spiritual world, bridging earth and Heaven.

At the end of my life, I was bedfast on oxygen in a hospital room. These were difficult months because my lungs collapsed, and I couldn't breathe on my own. As I was never guaranteed a long life, my parents were ready for the inevitable. They respected my living will by removing the oxygen and feeding tubes. During this time of physical confinement, my soul was able to leave and float through the hospital walls. Souls of other comatose patients were able to float around the hospital wing as well. We could greet each other and telepathically communicate. Even though these spirits had physical bodies in comatose states, their families wanted them to remain on earth. I sensed that some of them were very agitated, as their agreed upon time line was up. By being imprisoned in a body, so to speak, they couldn't go on to their next stage of life.

When my parents finally let me go, it was such a relief for me. My maternal grandfather was there to greet me on the other side. This spiritual world is not out in the darkness of space, where the stars are. This soul place is an overlapping dimension on earth, with a faster frequency. I had never physically met my grandpa because he had died before I was born. He later communicated to me that he was my spirit guide. For my entire life he was invisibly there more than I knew, to guide and help me.

When I first made transition I felt more *alive* than ever with just my light body that could soar, walk, run and shake hands. I was even capable of hugging others in Heaven! Then I agreed to move on to my life review.

During my review I was helped by my spirit guides and the Higher Consciousness to review my past life in an objective way. I remembered that I chose everything for my soul's advancement. And I recalled past lifetimes with my father who tried to control and dictate to me. In one past lifetime my father was an aggressive older brother, and in another lifetime he was a bossy first cousin. So I chose him as a father, knowing that even though he was a doctor there was nothing he could do for my chosen disabilities. I was free and independent of my father's control! Selecting my disabled health condition gave me that freedom. My parents loved me and I loved them, but the courage to fight obstacles *was* the soul lesson I chose to learn. My mind was always sharp and intact, even though I was physically disabled.

I remembered that we choose parents, siblings, places to be born, future children, lovers and even spouses from our soul group. Also the length of life on earth, called the "timeline," is pre-chosen. If a baby is born with medical problems or disabilities, please know that the soul chose that condition to spiritually advance. Possibly the family needed to learn faith or patience with their child's disability. Perhaps the soul itself needed to learn courage and self-assertion, as I did. I feel the soul choices we make are important to address. Families may feel that they are being punished by God for their child's condition. They may also feel that dire health conditions are from something that they did wrong. Please tell people to release guilt in regards to their family's disabilities. When the family finally returns to their soul group on this side, they will fully understand the deeper reason for the soul agreements that were made.

I also want to add that if a disabled health condition happens later in someone's life, it is no accident. For example, if a diver falls on his head at the age of 30 and becomes paralyzed, or a lady is thrown from a horse and is restricted in a wheelchair, their conditions have been pre-agreed to before their incarnations. Here we do not give credence to so-called accidents; we deem accidents as a chosen life event that is necessary for soul growth. Pre-chosen soul lessons are not only for the individual to progress, but also for those who surround the individual. If during an accident the soul's contracted timeline is *not* up, angels can intervene and save the individual. But if one's timeline is up, then that soul will return to this side.

It was an honor for me to share this information, and I hope it was helpful. I send blessings and goodwill to those on earth.

James

Many years ago, I was doing in-home group sessions. One of my favorite clients was a very sweet person named Debbie.

Debbie loved my first book which was called Visions from Mary. *In a vision the Blessed Mother appeared to me in 1993, even though I wasn't Catholic! Blessed Mother encouraged me to paint 12 paintings of the Madonna and write 12 accompanying chapters containing prayers and meditations. Debbie bought the book, removed the 12 colored prints and excitedly framed them. She really was one of the most loving and kindest ladies I have ever met. When she was in her 50s, Debbie developed diabetes, was kept in a wheelchair and had to have both of her legs amputated. Later her husband wrote to us and sadly shared that Debbie had passed away. I prayed for her family and for her soul to have peace in Heaven.*

One day while I was sitting and relaxing, I heard a familiar voice:

Hi, I hope you remember me. It's Debbie! From Heaven I can see your inner light. Please take care of yourself, because you are needed by so many. You helped me and my family believe in angels. You were an earth angel to us!

I want to talk about my health condition and how it affected me. At the age of 54 I became a diabetic. My legs hurt so much and were always swollen. I had severe edema, my circulation was cut off and both of my legs had to be amputated. It was tiresome to remain in my wheelchair. When I was young I was so active with my family, husband and son. I so missed my legs! I want to share with you that now in my heavenly home my light body is fully intact. My spirit can walk, run and even fly! My husband is lost without me because we were very close for many years. Your *Visions from Mary* book is beautiful, and the paintings from your book still hang on my living room wall.

I was ready to leave the earth, and my heart just gave out. If anyone reading this has lost limbs from a health condition or a war situation, tell them, "A car can lose its tires, like the physical body can lose its limbs, but the driver of the car remains intact, which is the spirit." One of my weaknesses was that I tended to be pushy with people. When I arrived here I remembered that I chose the diabetic condition in later life to learn humility. I had to listen to others and let them wait on me.

I thank you, Michele, for sending a "love donation" to me before I passed away. We never did get the elevator to let me go to the second floor of our house, but I'm in the Lord's house now. It's wonderful to be free from pain, dancing and praising Him!

Thanks for listening,
Debbie

20

A Soldier's Story

My husband and I live about an hour away from the Gettysburg, PA battlefield, where the Civil War battle of 1863 took place. The Union soldiers, called the Bluecoats of the North, were in battle with the Confederates soldiers called the Graycoats of the South. I knew some of the history of the Civil War but was not particularly drawn to that three-day massacre in Gettysburg.

One morning, after praying and meditating, I opened my eyes and saw a soldier! Across from me sat the spirit of a young man wearing a gray, tattered Confederate uniform with dirt on his boots. He appeared young and attractive, with light brown curly hair and bright blue eyes. I could tell he was anxious to relay his personal story about his experiences, and so it began:

My name is David Smith, and my last lifetime was during the Civil War era. I was from the border state of West Virginia, and I was drafted as a Confederate soldier at the age of 18.

Guess you could call me lucky on the battlefield that day in Gettysburg. I was instantly killed, shot through the heart and head, so I never knew what hit me. I was in no pain, and as my spirit rose above my dead body, I glanced down at the battlefield. There were bloody limbs everywhere and men were groaning and screaming out in pain. Some soldiers were crying for their beloved wives, children or families. Others just moaned and sobbed out of fear.

My good friend during the Civil War battle was on the front line with me. His name was Michael, and we were like "soul brothers" because neither one of us had a biological brother. We grew up together in the foothills of the Allegheny Mountains in West Virginia, a simple and happy life. I did not have a girlfriend in West Virginia because there wasn't much time for flirting, as I had lots of chores to do. Fun for us was fishing, climbing trees and hunting. I lived in a cabin, and my friend Mike lived about a mile away.

We were both 18 when the command came from General Lee for us to ride north towards Gettysburg, PA. It was July 1863 and a very hot spell was upon us. Mike and I weren't necessarily scared, but we didn't think we'd die. Mike was behind me when I was shot and died. He wasn't as lucky, as he then lost his left leg and lay in agony on the battlefield. By the time the medical team could give him any help, gangrene had set in and he died of complications. However, along with his favorite maternal grandma, Peg, I was there after Mike passed away to help him get to the light.

Since you're writing a book about this side, I thought you might like to know how it is from a soldier's viewpoint. Spirits who were soldiers can band together here, from different war times in history. On earth there are clubs like the American Legion and the VFW (Veterans of Foreign Wars). We don't have clubs in Heaven, but we can gather together to share "war stories." This does not mean that we all served in the same war. World War II Vets can communicate with us Civil War soldiers. Vietnam Vets can share stories with Korean War Vets.

I bring this up because war is a terrible thing. Those who die in war are scared and confused, and don't let anybody tell you different. When there has been a horrific war on earth, soldier spirits can group together to lend their support from Heaven. We are never forced to do anything, but a few war victims here try to influence the minds of those in military command and bring peace to your world. War on earth is for control, for religious beliefs, for power, for land and for greed.

Men who have been wounded before death may "wake up" here in makeshift hospitals, especially those who didn't believe in an afterlife. They open their spirit eyes to find smiling faces and kind, caring actions from other spirits. I must say that these medical beings were not necessarily doctors or nurses while on earth. They *choose* to help the new arrivals because of their compassion and concern. These new arrivals do not have physical bodies of course, so a formerly trained doctor is not necessary. What *is* necessary, it seems, is to help these spirits release any residue of fear and feel perfect peace.

The scenario of a hospital is not created for everyone who has passed in a war situation. It is created especially for those who are disoriented, fearful and confused because they were never told what to expect in the afterlife. But I myself went straight through the spiritual portal and right away met my loved ones and my dog, Shy. Shy was a coonhound and my best friend when I was growing up, so he was there waiting for me!

In this world, we are all perfectly formed. If a limb has been shot off during war, it is made whole. We can project to one another the way we want to look. There is no need to appear old or sick, so most of us will return to how we looked in our best years of age. Many spirits project at the age of the late 20s to early 30s. A baby or young child who has passed away can also project older if they wish to.

You might ask what I'm doing now to occupy my time. While some soldiers here want to learn from great military commanders, generals and strategists, I just want to know more about the workings of nature. I loved plants and I'm choosing to study about the plant kingdom with those who were botanists. There are classes in Heaven on every subject, and teachers are most valued. I have telepathically created a beautiful wildflower garden and pine trees with my thought forms. They are primarily herbal wildflower gardens with the flora and fauna that I knew and loved in West Virginia. I have not as yet decided what future time frame to be born into, but I've decided to be a botanist when I do. It's not that I don't like people, but I feel that nature is where the "Heart of God" truly is. *Nature* just *is*. Nature is not artificial, demanding or controlling. Its beauty lies within itself in an unassuming way.

I'm free now to enjoy lying on my back in my southern wildflower meadow and creating sunny days. I love to stare at the puffy white clouds above, just as I did as a child. I have no wish to learn about the dynamics of the universe, about science or advanced mathematics. I want to come back to earth with the knowledge I have learned about how to cultivate plants from great horticulturists and botanists. It would be interesting to even become a naturalist landscaper to fulfill that mission. There may be many opportunities to use what I've learned here during my next lifetime.

But for now there is no war, anger, pain or strife. Lying on my back, looking at clouds with my coonhound beside me will suffice!

David

Seeing death as the end of life is like seeing the horizon as the end of the ocean.

—David Searls

Epilogue

Hopefully you have read this book with an open mind and heart and are able to grasp the concept of physical death but not death of the soul.

Some individual soul accounts of the afterlife you may resonate with, while others will seem unbelievably extraordinary. Yet, I believe there truly is a light-filled place that awaits you where you will remember who you are as a spiritual being on an evolutionary journey. Once again you will return to your original home, celebrate loving reunions and feel the transcendent essence of perfect love and peace.

Michele Livingston

About the Author

Michele A. Livingston is an internationally known visionary, spiritual medium, gifted artist and inter-faith minister. With a master's degree in art education, she taught art in public schools and later displayed her work in her own art gallery. Clairvoyant from an early age, she has the incredible ability to see and communicate with departed loved ones and spirit guides. For the past 25 years, Michele has brought comfort and closure to those seeking answers from their loved ones in Heaven.

Michele has appeared on stage, doing "double links" with world renowned medium, James Van Praagh, who has called her a "trance channel" because of her ability to take on the personality of those with whom she is communicating. Michele is also one of only a handful of mediums, worldwide, endorsed by Van Praagh on his website.

Michele has touched thousands of people with one-on-one readings, seminars and personal appearances by providing messages and actual visions of their loved ones in the spirit realms. She has hosted her own radio talk show, had her own TV show and has made numerous other appearances on radio and TV. As a healer and counselor, she continues to bring messages and soul-healing stories to people all over the globe as she assists them in taking that "next step" in consciousness to become closer to the Creator.

Michele is available for radio and TV interviews, seminars, group sessions, phone and in-person consultations. For more information on Michele Livingston please visit her website at: http://www.michelelivingston.com, or call (717) 737-3888.

Made in the USA
Middletown, DE
08 November 2022

14437192R00104